Game Development with Three.js

Embrace the next generation of game development
and reach millions of gamers online with the Three.js
3D graphics library

Isaac Sukin

PUBLISHING

BIRMINGHAM - MUMBAI

Game Development with Three.js

First published: October 2013

Production Reference: 1171013

Published by Packt Publishing Ltd.
Livery Place
35 Livery Street
Birmingham B3 2PB, UK.

ISBN 978-1-78216-853-9

www.packtpub.com

Cover Image by Suresh Mogre (suresh.mogre.99@gmail.com)

Credits

Author
Isaac Sukin

Reviewers
Ian Langworth
Wenli Zhang

Acquisition Editor
Gregory Wild

Commissioning Editor
Govindan K

Technical Editors
Arwa Manasawala
Veena Pagare

Project Coordinator
Aboli Ambardekar

Proofreader
Jonathan Todd

Indexer
Mehreen Deshmukh

Production Coordinator
Arvindkumar Gupta

Cover Work
Arvindkumar Gupta

About the Author

Isaac Sukin has been building games since he was eight years old, when he discovered that Nerf Arena Blast came with a copy of Epic Games' Unreal Editor. At 16, he became co-leader of the Community Bonus Pack team, an international group of game developers for the Unreal Engine that won 49 awards over the next few years. He started learning to code around the same time by developing an open source Facebook-style statuses system that thousands of websites have adopted. Since then, he has been increasingly drawn to interactive JavaScript on the web. He created an open source 2D game engine in early 2012 and then dove into Three.js.

As of 2013, he is a senior, studying entrepreneurship and information management at the Wharton school at the University of Pennsylvania. He has worked for Twitter, First Round Capital, and Acquia among others, and was previously a freelance consultant and developer. He is also a founder of Dorm Room Fund, a student-run venture capital fund that invests in student-run startups. You can find him on GitHub and Twitter under the alias IceCreamYou or visit his website at www.isaacsukin.com.

He has previously published short stories and poetry, but this is his first book.

Thanks, Mom and Dad, for your love and support in exploring my passions. To Lauren and Sarah, I am so proud to have such amazing little sisters. I love you.

And a shout out to the CBP3 team! Thanks for a lot of fun over the years.

About the Reviewers

Ian Langworth is the co-founder and CTO of Artillery, which aims to bring console-quality games to the browser using HTML5, WebGL, and other cutting-edge browser technology. Prior to Artillery, he was the first engineering hire at Redbeacon (acquired by The Home Depot in 2012), and before that he was a software engineer at Google. He is the co-author of *Perl Testing: A Developer's Notebook*, O'Reilly, 2005.

Wenli Zhang is a graduate student at Digital Art Lab of Shanghai Jiao Tong University. She has sufficient experience in web design and programming and shows great interest in it. She's familiar with HTML, CSS, JavaScript, Three.js, jQuery, PHP, and so on. She's also interested in graphics rendering and image processing.

She originally learned Three.js for a game to demonstrate web audio during her internship in Intel corp. Owing to her knowledge in the field of computer graphics and previous experience with OpenGL, she learned Three.js quickly and developed a 3D Arcalands game within a week. After that, she used Three.js for several applications and found it efficient and easy to use.

She has also developed a jQuery plugin named jWebAudio (`http://01org.github.io/jWebAudio/`), which is a web audio library designed for games.

Her personal site is `http://ovilia.github.com`.

www.PacktPub.com

Support files, eBooks, discount offers and more

You might want to visit `www.PacktPub.com` for support files and downloads related to your book.

Did you know that Packt offers eBook versions of every book published, with PDF and ePub files available? You can upgrade to the eBook version at `www.PacktPub.com` and as a print book customer, you are entitled to a discount on the eBook copy. Get in touch with us at `service@packtpub.com` for more details.

At `www.PacktPub.com`, you can also read a collection of free technical articles, sign up for a range of free newsletters and receive exclusive discounts and offers on Packt books and eBooks.

`http://PacktLib.PacktPub.com`

Do you need instant solutions to your IT questions? PacktLib is Packt's online digital book library. Here, you can access, read and search across Packt's entire library of books.

Why Subscribe?

- Fully searchable across every book published by Packt
- Copy and paste, print and bookmark content
- On demand and accessible via web browser

Free Access for Packt account holders

If you have an account with Packt at `www.PacktPub.com`, you can use this to access PacktLib today and view nine entirely free books. Simply use your login credentials for immediate access.

Table of Contents

Preface

Three.js is an easy-to-learn 3D graphics library for the web. This book explains the Three.js API and how to use it to build immersive online games. By the time you finish this book, you'll be able to reach millions of gamers through their web browsers, and you'll build exciting projects such as a first-person shooter along the way.

I've been building games for more than a decade. When I discovered Three.js, the first project I built was very similar to the first-person shooter game you'll build in *Chapter 3, Exploring and Interacting*. I was hooked by how quickly I could create fun games with no prior exposure to the library.

In *Game Development with Three.js*, I've tried to stay true to that exploratory spirit. I hope you have as much fun reading it as I had writing it.

What this book covers

Chapter 1, Hello, Three.js, describes what Three.js is and what it does, how to start writing code with it, and a basic scene.

Chapter 2, Building a World, explains the components of a Three.js scene including renderers, geometries, materials, and lighting for building a procedurally generated city.

Chapter 3, Exploring and Interacting, explains mouse and keyboard interaction, basic physics, and creating a first-person shooter game.

Chapter 4, Adding Detail, explains particle systems, sound, graphic effects, and managing external assets such as 3D models in addition to building a capture-the-flag game.

Chapter 5, Design and Development, describes game design for the web, including development processes, performance considerations, and the basics of networking.

What you need for this book

You will need a web browser. To fully experience all the features discussed in this book, use Chrome 22 or later or Firefox 22 or later. Internet Explorer 11 or later should also work. A text editor is also recommended, especially if you are not using Chrome, as discussed in *Chapter 1, Hello, Three.js*. You will need an Internet connection at certain points in the book such as when downloading the Three.js library (these points will be identified in the text).

Who this book is for

This book is for people interested in programming 3D games for the web. Basic familiarity with JavaScript syntax and a basic understanding of HTML and CSS is assumed. No prior exposure to Three.js is assumed. This book should be useful regardless of prior experience with game programming, whether you intend to build casual side projects or large-scale professional titles.

Conventions

In this book, you will find a number of styles of text that distinguish between different kinds of information. Here are some examples of these styles, and an explanation of their meaning.

Code words in text, database table names, folder names, filenames, file extensions, pathnames, dummy URLs, user input, and Twitter handles are shown as follows: "The THREE variable is global."

A block of code is set as follows:

```
renderer = new THREE.CanvasRenderer();
renderer.setSize(window.innerWidth, window.innerHeight);
document.body.appendChild(renderer.domElement);
```

When we wish to draw your attention to a particular part of a code block, the relevant lines or items are set in bold:

```
renderer = new THREE.WebGLRenderer();
renderer.setSize(window.innerWidth, window.innerHeight);
document.body.appendChild(renderer.domElement);
```

New terms and **important words** are shown in bold. Words that you see on the screen, in menus or dialog boxes for example, appear in the text like this: "If you want to experiment with WebGL features that are still in development, you can enable some of them in Canary's **about:flags** page."

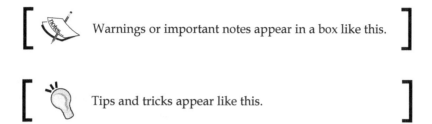

Warnings or important notes appear in a box like this.

Tips and tricks appear like this.

Reader feedback

Feedback from our readers is always welcome. Let us know what you think about this book—what you liked or may have disliked. Reader feedback is important for us to develop titles that you really get the most out of.

To send us general feedback, simply send an e-mail to feedback@packtpub.com, and mention the book title via the subject of your message.

If there is a topic that you have expertise in and you are interested in either writing or contributing to a book, see our author guide on www.packtpub.com/authors.

Customer support

Now that you are the proud owner of a Packt book, we have a number of things to help you to get the most from your purchase.

Downloading the example code

You can download the example code files for all Packt books you have purchased from your account at http://www.packtpub.com. If you purchased this book elsewhere, you can visit http://www.packtpub.com/support and register to have the files e-mailed directly to you.

Downloading the color images of this book

We also provide you a PDF file that has color images of the screenshots/diagrams used in this book. The color images will help you better understand the changes in the output. You can download this file from `http://www.packtpub.com/sites/default/files/downloads/8539OS_Images.pdf`

Errata

Although we have taken every care to ensure the accuracy of our content, mistakes do happen. If you find a mistake in one of our books—maybe a mistake in the text or the code—we would be grateful if you would report this to us. By doing so, you can save other readers from frustration and help us improve subsequent versions of this book. If you find any errata, please report them by visiting `http://www.packtpub.com/submit-errata`, selecting your book, clicking on the **errata submission form** link, and entering the details of your errata. Once your errata are verified, your submission will be accepted and the errata will be uploaded on our website, or added to any list of existing errata, under the Errata section of that title. Any existing errata can be viewed by selecting your title from `http://www.packtpub.com/support`.

Piracy

Piracy of copyright material on the Internet is an ongoing problem across all media. At Packt, we take the protection of our copyright and licenses very seriously. If you come across any illegal copies of our works, in any form, on the Internet, please provide us with the location address or website name immediately so that we can pursue a remedy.

Please contact us at `copyright@packtpub.com` with a link to the suspected pirated material.

We appreciate your help in protecting our authors, and our ability to bring you valuable content.

Questions

You can contact us at `questions@packtpub.com` if you are having a problem with any aspect of the book, and we will do our best to address it.

1
Hello, Three.js

This chapter will take you from zero to sixty with a new Three.js project. We'll cover what Three.js is, how to get started with writing code for it, and the components of a basic scene.

The wonderful world of Three.js

Three.js is a JavaScript library that simplifies displaying 3D graphics in web browsers. Artists, major brands, and many others are increasingly using Three.js to power immersive online experiences that can reach millions of people across many platforms. There are many inspiring demos of the technology at `http://threejs.org/`.

Three.js is usually used with a new technology called **WebGL**, a JavaScript API for rendering graphics without plugins. The API is based on **OpenGL**, a desktop graphics API (**GL** stands for **graphics library**). Because it uses the client's graphics processing unit to accelerate rendering, WebGL is fast! However, many mobile browsers as well as Internet Explorer 10 and below do not support WebGL. Luckily, Three.js supports rendering with the **HTML5 Canvas API** as well as other technologies such as **Scalable Vector Graphics** instead.

 You can find up-to-date information on browser support at `http://caniuse.com/webgl`.

Three.js is originally written and maintained by *Ricardo Cabello,* who is also known as *Mr.Doob.* The library is open source (MIT-licensed) and is available from its GitHub page, `https://github.com/mrdoob/three.js`. The documentation of Three.js is available online at `http://threejs.org/docs/`. When the documentation is insufficient, the best place to look is the `examples` folder of the project, which contains a large collection of examples demonstrating different features. You can browse the examples online at `http://threejs.org/examples/`. The source code in the `src` folder is also worth browsing if you need to know how a certain class works or what methods and properties it exposes. Developers respond to questions about Three.js on the Q&A site **StackOverflow**, so if you are confused about something, you can browse questions with the `three.js` tag or ask your own.

 This book was written with Version r61 of the Three.js project. Certain parts of the API are still under development, but anything that is likely to change will be pointed out when it is introduced.

Let's code!

Because Three.js runs in web browsers, it can run on—and be developed on—many different platforms. In fact, we're going to build our first Three.js project directly in a browser!

Open up `http://mrdoob.com/projects/htmleditor/`. You should see HTML and JavaScript code overlaid on top of a spinning sphere-like shape, as shown in the following screenshot:

```
1   <!DOCTYPE html>
2   <html>
3       <head>
4           <meta charset="utf-8">
5           <style>
6               body {
7                   background-color: #ffffff;
8                   margin: 0;
9                   overflow: hidden;
10              }
11          </style>
12      </head>
13      <body>
14          <script src="http://mrdoob.github.com/three.js/build/three
15          <script>
16
17              var camera, scene, renderer;
18              var geometry, material, mesh;
19
20              init();
```

The online Three.js editor

This is the `Hello, World` program of Three.js—the minimum code required to get a spinning shape rendering in the browser. The preview will automatically update when you change any code, so go ahead and play with it and see what happens. For example, try changing `THREE.MeshBasicMaterial` to `THREE.MeshNormalMaterial`. What happens if you change `IcosahedronGeometry` to `TorusKnotGeometry`? Try fiddling with some numbers. Can you make the shape rotate faster or slower?

Been there, scene that

Let's dig deeper into our spinning-shape world and explain how it all works. You can follow along with this section in the online editor or type the code into a new HTML file.

First, there's the HTML template:

```html
<!DOCTYPE html>
<html>
  <head>
    <meta charset="utf-8">
    <style>
      body {
        background-color: #ffffff;
        margin: 0;
        overflow: hidden;
      }
    </style>
  </head>
  <body>
    <script src="http://mrdoob.github.com/three.js/build/three.min.js"></script>
    <script> /* …your code here… */ </script>
  </body>
</html>
```

Nothing surprising here. We're basically just including Three.js and removing the browser's default page margins. The `<canvas>` element, onto which we'll render our scene, will be added into the DOM by our JavaScript.

 Instead of using the Three.js file from the GitHub CDN, you should download the latest Three.js build and include the local copy in your projects. The full Three.js script can be found in the `build` folder of the project or can be downloaded from `https://raw.github.com/mrdoob/three.js/master/build/three.js`. In production, you will want to use the minified version (`three.min.js`).

Now comes the fun part: telling Three.js to display something. First, let's declare the objects we'll need:

```
var camera, scene, renderer;
var geometry, material, mesh;
```

Then, let's give them values and explain what they do:

```
scene = new THREE.Scene();
```

A `Scene` class represents a list of objects that affect what is displayed on the screen, such as 3D models and lights. (Each class provided by Three.js is invoked as a property of the global `THREE` variable.) A scene isn't very useful by itself, so let's put something in it.

Downloading the example code

You can download the example code files for all Packt books you have purchased from your account at `http://www.packtpub.com`. If you purchased this book elsewhere, you can visit `http://www.packtpub.com/support` and register to have the files e-mailed directly to you.

A `mesh` object can be displayed in a scene, instantiated using the `THREE.Mesh` constructor. It consists of `geometry`, which is the object's shape, and a `material`, which is a color, image, or other texture that defines how the faces of the shape appear. In this case, the geometry we'll use is `IcosahedronGeometry`, which is based on a 20-sided shape approximating a sphere. The constructor takes a radius and detail, where detail is the number of times to split each edge of the icosahedron to add more faces and make the shape closer to a sphere:

```
geometry = new THREE.IcosahedronGeometry(200, 1);
material = new THREE.MeshBasicMaterial({ color: 0x000000, wireframe:
true, wireframeLinewidth: 2 });
mesh = new THREE.Mesh(geometry, material);
```

`MeshBasicMaterial` is a type of material that is not affected by the surrounding lighting. The options we're passing include the color in hex format (like you'd use in CSS), whether to display the shape as a solid color or highlight the edges, and how thick to draw the wireframe, respectively.

There are many other types of geometry and materials. *Chapter 2, Building a World* describes them in detail.

Now we can add our mesh to the scene:

```
scene.add(mesh);
```

We've put together what we want to display, so the next step is to actually display it. Three.js accomplishes this with **renderers**, which take the objects in a scene, perform some calculations, and then ask the browser to display the result in a specific format like WebGL. The renderer creates a new `<canvas>` element by default that should be added to the DOM:

```
renderer = new THREE.CanvasRenderer();
renderer.setSize(window.innerWidth, window.innerHeight);
document.body.appendChild(renderer.domElement);
```

Here, we're using the `CanvasRenderer` as our method of displaying the scene. (We'll cover other renderers such as `WebGLRenderer` in *Chapter 2, Building a World*.) We're also telling the renderer to display the scene at the full size of the browser window with our `setSize()` call. Then we will add the renderer's canvas to the DOM with `appendChild(renderer.domElement)`.

Avoid changing the canvas' size with CSS; use the renderer's `setSize` method instead, which sets the `width` and `height` HTML attributes on the canvas element. This is because CSS describes the display size but not the render size. That is, if the canvas is rendered at 800 x 600, but the CSS shows it at 1024 x 768, the rendering will be stretched to fill the space just like if you specified the CSS size of an image to be larger than its true size. This can result in distortion and difficulty converting between "screen space" and "canvas space."

The one last thing we need is a `camera` object as shown in the following code snippet, which is something Three.js uses to tell the renderer from what perspective the scene should be displayed. If the player was standing in your virtual world and their screen represented what they could see, `camera` would be their eyes, `renderer` would be their brain, and `scene` would be their universe.

```
camera = new THREE.PerspectiveCamera(75, window.innerWidth / window.
innerHeight, 1, 1000);
camera.position.z = 500;
```

A `PerspectiveCamera` instance displays the world from a single point in space, just like your eyes. This creates a little bit of distortion due to distance (objects that are farther away appear smaller). There is also an `OrthographicCamera` class which is like looking out from a plane. Orthographic cameras are sometimes used for **isometric** (also known as **2.5D**) games and level editors to get accurate views of objects' relative sizes. You can see the difference in the following figure:

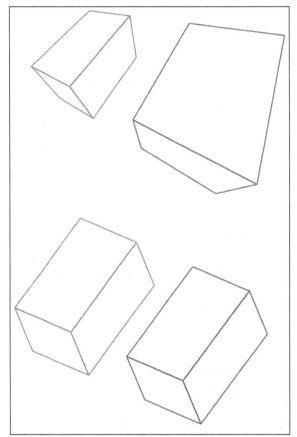

Camera projections. Top is perspective and bottom is orthographic.

The `PerspectiveCamera` object's parameters are field of view (in degrees), which controls how wide the camera lens is; aspect ratio, the ratio of the canvas' width to its height; near-plane frustum, the closest an object can be to the camera and still be seen; and far-plane frustum, the farthest an object can be from the camera and still be rendered. You'll rarely need to change these values

Also notice that we change the camera's location by assigning to `camera.position.z`. Three.js uses a **spatial coordinate system** in which, by default, the x-axis increases from left to right, the z-axis increases from back to front, and the y-axis increases upward. Most objects have a *position* and *scale*, both of which are represented by a three-dimensional vector (specifically `THREE.Vector3`). They also have a *rotation* represented by a `THREE.Euler` instance, which is an abstraction that allows treating rotation much like a vector. All objects are initialized at the position (0, 0, 0), also called the **origin**. Rotation also starts at (0, 0, 0), and scale starts at (1, 1, 1). Vectors are very versatile, but usually all you'll need to do with them is assign to the x, y, and z properties. For example, if we wanted to move the camera upward, we could increase `camera.position.y`.

Finally, we can display the scene by asking the renderer to display it from the camera's perspective:

```
renderer.render(scene, camera);
```

Hooray, a static 3D display! If you have been following along by rebuilding our scene from scratch, now is the point at which you can actually see the results of your work. Just open the HTML file in a browser. (If you're loading the `three.js` file from GitHub instead of locally, you'll need to be connected to the Internet.)

A static scene isn't very fun though, so let's add animation by constructing a render loop:

```
animate();

function animate() {

  requestAnimationFrame(animate);

  mesh.rotation.x = Date.now() * 0.00005;
  mesh.rotation.y = Date.now() * 0.0001;

  renderer.render(scene, camera);

}
```

The key here is `requestAnimationFrame()`, which executes the function passed to it when the browser is ready to paint a new frame. In that function, we perform any necessary updates to the scene (in this case, changing the mesh's `rotation` vector just like we changed the camera's `position` vector earlier) and then ask the renderer to repaint the canvas as before.

Putting it all together (and also wrapping our setup code in a function for clarity), we get:

```javascript
var camera, scene, renderer;
var geometry, material, mesh;

init();
animate();

function init() {

  camera = new THREE.PerspectiveCamera( 75, window.innerWidth /
  window.innerHeight, 1, 1000 );
  camera.position.z = 500;

  scene = new THREE.Scene();

  geometry = new THREE.IcosahedronGeometry( 200, 1 );
  material = new THREE.MeshBasicMaterial( { color: 0x000000,
  wireframe: true, wireframeLinewidth: 2 } );

  mesh = new THREE.Mesh( geometry, material );
  scene.add( mesh );

  renderer = new THREE.CanvasRenderer();
  renderer.setSize( window.innerWidth, window.innerHeight );

  document.body.appendChild( renderer.domElement );

}

function animate() {

  requestAnimationFrame( animate );

  mesh.rotation.x = Date.now() * 0.00005;
  mesh.rotation.y = Date.now() * 0.0001;

  renderer.render( scene, camera );

}
```

It's animating! You've now built your first 3D world in the browser. Because it's in JavaScript, you can also easily send it to your friends. (In the online editor, click on the stacked bars icon ☰ at the upper-right, click on the **Download** button, and then rename the downloaded file with a .html extension.)

> Both within the Three.js repository and online, most of the Three.js examples you'll find will have all their code in a single HTML file. This is convenient for small projects but unhealthy for larger ones. Even though most of the code in this book is small enough to be manageable in a single file, we will try to use patterns that make the code maintainable. *Chapter 5, Design and Development* specifically addresses designs that work well at scale.

Choosing your environment

The Google Chrome browser is usually considered to be on the leading edge of WebGL support, so many Three.js developers work mainly in either the latest stable version of Chrome or the alpha-release branch, named **Canary**. Chrome has a lot of other advantages too, such as advanced performance profiling, the ability to emulate touch events, and support for inspecting canvas frames. (You can access these features through the Chrome Developer Tools settings. Canvas inspection is explained well at http://www.html5rocks.com/en/tutorials/canvas/inspection/.) If you want to experiment with WebGL features that are still in development, you can enable some of them in Canary's **about:flags** page.

When it comes to coding, the online Three.js editor is great for testing small, isolated concepts, but it quickly gets cumbersome for more complex projects. Most programming environments have solid JavaScript support, but some are better than others.

Chrome also has a script-editing environment that works well for some people. If you open the Chrome Developer Tools (*Ctrl / Cmd + Shift + I*) and switch to the **Sources** tab, you can configure Chrome to edit files from your local filesystem. This environment includes syntax highlighting, debugging, autocompletion, source mapping for minified files, revision control that visually shows changes, and the ability to run the code instantly without reloading the page. Additionally, you can store snippets for reuse as described at https://developers.google.com/chrome-developer-tools/docs/authoring-development-workflow#snippets.

You can see what the editor looks like in the following screenshot:

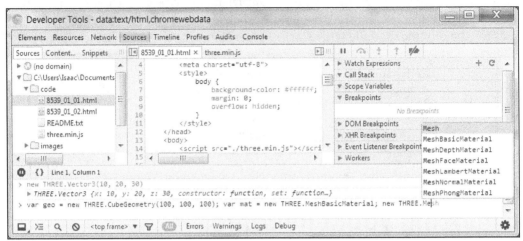

Google Chrome Developer Tools

If you prefer to work outside of the Chrome editor, it can be tedious to constantly switch windows and reload the page. There are several tools that attempt to solve this. LiveReload (http://livereload.com/) and Tin.cr (http://tin.cr/) are the best known; they are browser extensions that automatically reload the page when you save a file. You may also want to try LightTable (http://www.lighttable.com/), an experimental IDE that also autoreloads and additionally includes tools for visually manipulating your code.

If you use Sublime Text as your editor, you can install autocompletion support for Three.js commands through the package manager or from the Three.js repository itself (in /utils/editors).

Summary

We have constructed our first 3D world with Three.js. In this chapter, we learned what Three.js is and does, reviewed the basic components of a Three.js scene, and set up our editing environment. We used the scene, renderer, camera, mesh, geometry, and material components for the first time.

In the next chapter, we will cover these components in more detail, including the different kinds of the renderer, geometry, and material components. We will also add lighting to the mix and make a more advanced scene.

2
Building a World

This chapter explains the components of a Three.js scene in detail, including the different kinds of renderers, geometries, materials, and lighting. We will also build a procedurally generated city.

Geometries

Geometries are instances of `THREE.Geometry` that define the shape of an object in a scene. They are made up of vertices and faces (which are themselves objects and are accessible through the `vertices` and `faces` array properties). Vertices are the `THREE.Vector3` objects representing points in three-dimensional space, while faces are the `THREE.Face3` objects representing triangular surfaces. (All more complex shapes are subdivided into triangular faces for rendering purposes.)

Luckily, dealing with vertices and faces directly is usually unnecessary because `THREE.Geometry` has many subclasses that help create commonly used shapes.

3D primitives

Three.js provides a number of classes that generate common shapes. The official documentation for each type is available at `http://threejs.org/docs/`, but a summary of common types is shown in the following table (some obscure, optional constructor parameters were omitted):

Type	Constructor	Description
Cube	`THREE.CubeGeometry(width, height, depth, widthSegments = 1, heightSegments = 1, depthSegments = 1)`	It is a rectangular box with the specified dimensions. The `segments` parameters split the sides into smaller rectangles.

Type	Constructor	Description

Sphere	`THREE.Sphere(radius,`
	`horizontalSegments = 8,`
	`verticalSegments = 6)`
		It is a sphere approximation created by calculating segments.

Polyhedra (spheroids)	`THREE.Icosahedron(radius,`
	`detail = 0);`
	`THREE.Octahedron(radius,`
	`detail = 0);`
	`THREE.Tetrahedron(radius,`
	`detail = 0);`
		It is a sphere approximation based on shapes with 20, 8, or 4 sides, respectively; the `detail` parameter specifies how many times to split each edge to make more faces, making the shape more spherical.

Cylinder	`THREE.`
	`CylinderGeometry(radiusTop,`
	`radiusBottom, height,`
	`radiusSegments = 8,`
	`heightSegments = 1, openEnded`
	`= false)`
		`radiusSegments` is the number of edges connecting the top and bottom faces, down the curved surface; `heightSegments` is the number of rings of faces around the curved surface, and if `openEnded` is `true`, the ends of the cylinder will not be rendered.

Torus	`THREE.TorusGeometry(radius,`
	`tubeWidth = 40, radialSegments`
	`= 8, tubularSegments = 6)`
		It is a donut shape.

TorusKnot	`THREE.`
	`TorusKnotGeometry(radius,`
	`tubeWidth = 40,`
	`radialSegments,`
	`tubularSegments, p = 2, q = 3,`
	`heightScale = 1)`
		It is a knot shape, sort of like a pretzel. p and q are integers that affect how many twists are in the knot.

You can try changing the spinning icosahedron example we built in the last chapter to use different geometries by changing the `IcosahedronGeometry` constructor to one of the options in the preceding table. There is also a geometry viewer at `http://threejsplaygnd.brangerbriz.net/gui/` that allows you to tweak the constructor parameters to see the result and also copy the code required to generate the shape you're viewing.

2D primitives

Three.js also has default geometry for 2D shapes as shown in the following table:

Type	Constructor	Explanation
Plane	THREE.PlaneGeometry(width, height, widthSegments = 1, heightSegments = 1)	It is a rectangle with the specified dimensions. The segments parameters subdivide the plane into smaller rectangles.
Circle	THREE.CircleGeometry(radius, numberOfSides = 8)	It is a regular polygon.
Ring	THREE.RingGeometry(innerRadius, outerRadius, radialSegments = 8, ringSegments = 8)	It is a circle with a hole in the middle.

These shapes are created along the x and y axes by default.

Additionally, Three.js can create lines. Almost all objects you would normally place in a scene will be meshes, but lines are exceptions. Consider code like the following, which creates a mesh:

```
geometry = new THREE.IcosahedronGeometry(200, 2);
material = new THREE.MeshBasicMaterial({color: 0x000000});
mesh = new THREE.Mesh(geometry, material);
```

Instead of using the preceding code, you could use the code as shown in the following snippet to create a line:

```
geometry = new THREE.IcosahedronGeometry(200, 2);
material = new THREE.LineBasicMaterial({color: 0x000000});
mesh = new THREE.Line(geometry, material);
```

This can create some strange results for standard geometry such as IcosahedronGeometry because lines will be drawn connecting points in an unexpected order. Instead, you will usually want to create a custom geometry so that you can add vertices in your desired order.

[Use LineDashedMaterial instead of LineBasicMaterial to make a dotted line.]

Custom geometries

Several default geometry types allow creating shapes based on vertices or paths specifically created by the developer. (You can also import geometry created in external programs, a topic covered in *Chapter 4, Adding Detail*.) The most basic type is the THREE.Geometry class itself. For example, you can create a triangle using the code shown in the following snippet:

```
var geo = new THREE.Geometry();
geo.vertices = [
  new THREE.Vector3(0, 0, 0),
  new THREE.Vector3(0, 100, 0),
  new THREE.Vector3(0, 0, 100)
];
geo.faces.push(new THREE.Face3(0, 1, 2));
geo.computeBoundingSphere();
```

First, this code creates a geometry object that has no vertices or faces yet. Then, it adds specific vertices, where each vertex is represented by a THREE.Vector3 that holds spatial coordinates on the x, y, and z axes. Next, a THREE.Face3 is added into the faces array. The Face3 constructor's parameters indicate the indices of vertices in the geometry's vertices array to use for the face's corners. Finally, the bounding sphere is computed, which triggers internal calculations for properties Three.js needs to track such as whether the shape is in view. If you have trouble getting a texture to display correctly on your custom material, you may also need to call geo.computeFaceNormals() and geo.computeVertexNormals(). These functions calculate additional information about the geometry's visual layout.

Manually creating shapes out of individual vertices can quickly get tiring; however, some utilities exist to help make the process faster as introduced in the following table:

Geometry	Description
THREE.LatheGeometry	It revolves a shape in a circle
THREE.PolyhedronGeometry	A spheroid; examples include IcosahedronGeometry, TetrahedronGeometry, and so on
THREE.ExtrudeGeometry	It starts with a 2D shape and stretches it into a 3D space
THREE.ShapeGeometry	It is a 2D shape
THREE.TubeGeometry	It is a hollow cylinder
THREE.ParametricGeometry	These are curved tubes

Let's take extruding as an example since that's a relatively common operation:

```
var triangle = new THREE.Shape([
  new THREE.Vector2 (0,  50),
  new THREE.Vector2 (50, 50),
  new THREE.Vector2 (50,  0)
]);
var geometry = new THREE.ExtrudeGeometry(triangle, {
  bevelEnabled: false,
  amount: 30
});
```

The approach here is to create a 2D shape (THREE.Shape) out of (x, y) coordinates and then stretch it out along the z axis. The second parameter for ExtrudeGeometry is a map of options. The most important one, amount, controls how far to stretch out the shape. bevelEnabled controls whether the extruded edges are rounded or not. You can see the result in the following screenshot:

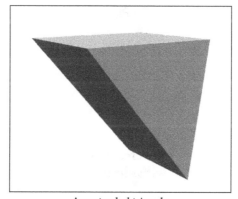

An extruded triangle

Use cases for the other custom geometries are unusual in games because normally if you wanted to create a complex shape, you could create a model in a 3D modeling program and then import it into Three.js (a process covered in *Chapter 4, Adding Detail*).

There is a WebGL-only class called THREE.BufferGeometry which is faster than THREE.Geometry, but is much more difficult to work with because it stores WebGL buffers instead of Three.js vertices and faces. However, future developments in Three.js will shift the default geometry to work more like THREE.BufferGeometry under the hood so that you don't have to think about the differences.

Text

Three.js can render text in 3D using geometry as well. To use this feature, you must include the font files after the Three.js library, but before your own code. For example, include the Helvetiker font using the following code:

```
<script src="https://raw.github.com/mrdoob/three.js/master/examples/
fonts/helvetiker_bold.typeface.js"></script>
<script src="https://raw.github.com/mrdoob/three.js/master/examples/
fonts/helvetiker_regular.typeface.js"></script>
```

(In production projects, you should download the fonts you want to use and include them locally.)

Three.js comes with several fonts in the `examples/fonts` directory. Custom fonts must be in the `typeface.js` format (you can convert OpenType and TrueType fonts to Typeface format at `http://typeface.neocracy.org/fonts.html`). Use the following code to create text geometry:

```
new THREE.TextGeometry("Text message goes here", {
  size: 30,
  height: 20, // extrude thickness
  font: "helvetiker", // font family in lower case
  weight: "normal", // or e.g. bold
  style: "normal", // or e.g. italics
  bevelEnabled: false
});
```

The `THREE.TextGeometry` constructor creates a shape representing the text in 2D, and then extrudes it as we did with our triangle. You can see the result in the following screenshot:

3D text

Materials

Materials are instances of THREE.Material that define how objects appear. There are several common material subclasses:

Constructor	Explanation
MeshBasicMaterial 	It is not affected by lighting (a characteristic called **unlit**), so this is usually used to display a solid color or a wireframe. Two adjacent, same-colored, unlit surfaces are difficult to tell apart.
MeshNormalMaterial 	The red/green/blue values of the colors displayed by this material are based on the magnitude of the x/y/z values of the faces' normal vectors. (A *normal* vector is perpendicular to a surface.) This material is unlit and useful for quickly distinguishing the shape of an object.
MeshDepthMaterial 	It is an unlit material that shows shades of gray, with brightness depending on the distance from the camera. It is useful when designing scenes before applying more realistic textures.
MeshLambertMaterial 	Faces are affected by lighting, but are not shiny. Specifically, lighting is calculated per-vertex and is interpolated over faces. It will appear black if there are no lights in the scene.
MeshPhongMaterial 	Faces are affected by lighting, and can be shiny. Specifically, lighting is calculated per-*texel* (texture pixel), so this will be more accurate than Lambert materials when the light source is close to the object in question. It will appear black if there are no lights in the scene.

Constructor	Explanation
MeshFaceMaterial 	It is essentially an array of materials used to map different materials to different surfaces. This material is unique in that instantiating it is different than all the others, as you can see in the following code:

```
var mat1 = new THREE.MeshPhongMaterial({ color:
0x0000ff });
var mat2 = new THREE.MeshPhongMaterial({ color:
0xff0000 });
var mat3 = new THREE.MeshPhongMaterial({ color:
0xffffff });
var materials = [mat1, mat2, mat3];
material = new THREE.
MeshFaceMaterial(materials);
for (var i = 0, l = geometry.faces.length; i <
l; i++) {
   geometry.faces[i].materialIndex = i % l;
}
```

Here, we create three new materials we want to use, pass them in an array to `MeshFaceMaterial`, and then set each face on our geometry to an index of the `materials` array that corresponds to the material we want for that face.

Constructor	Explanation
ShaderMaterial 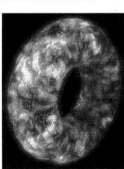	It displays a **GLSL (open Graphics Library Shading Language)** texture. GLSL is a programming language based on C that is used by WebGL and OpenGL to provide developers with a high-level, platform-agnostic way to control graphics. It is quite powerful and will be addressed more in *Chapter 4, Adding Detail*.

All of these material constructors except `MeshFaceMaterial` take a map of options as their only parameter. We've already encountered three options from our icosahedron example: `color`, `wireframe`, and `wireframeLinewidth`. Additionally, setting the `transparency` option to `true` allows use of the `opacity` option, a value between zero and one indicating how see-through the material should be (zero is invisible, one is opaque). For materials that don't use images, the other option that may be relevant is `shading`, which has a value of either `THREE.SmoothShading` or `THREE.FlatShading` indicating whether to blend colors of each face together, as shown in the next screenshot:

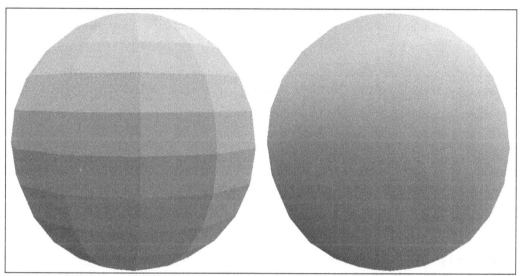

Left, THREE.MeshNormalMaterial({shading: THREE.FlatShading}); Right, THREE.
MeshNormalMaterial({shading: THREE.SmoothShading});

There are several other properties, the most important of which is also the most useful: `map`. This defines the texture used to wrap over the geometry. Usually, using this property looks like the following code snippet:

```
var image = THREE.ImageUtils.loadTexture('image.jpg');
new THREE.MeshBasicMaterial({map: image});
```

There are two issues to watch out for when loading images. First, if you are running your application locally (by double-clicking on the file, you will see a `file:///` URL), Chrome will prevent loading images by default for security reasons (to keep malicious JavaScript from accessing local files on your computer). You can solve this by either changing your browser's security settings or running the file using a local HTTP server as explained at `https://github.com/mrdoob/three.js/wiki/How-to-run-things-locally`. The second issue is that you cannot render images loaded from another domain in WebGL, also for security reasons. You can solve this by serving the image with the `Access-Control-Allow-Origin` header set to `null` as explained at `https://hacks.mozilla.org/2011/11/using-cors-to-load-webgl-textures-from-cross-domain-images/`.

The `ImageUtils.loadTexture()` function loads images. Let's use a slightly more advanced version to render the `earth` image:

```
THREE.ImageUtils.loadTexture('earth.jpg', undefined, function(texture)
{
  geometry = new THREE.SphereGeometry(280, 20, 20);
  material = new THREE.MeshBasicMaterial({map: texture, overdraw:
true});
  mesh = new THREE.Mesh(geometry, material);
  mesh.rotation.x = 30 * Math.PI / 180;
  scene.add(mesh);
});
```

The second parameter for `loadTexture` is currently unused, and the third parameter is a callback that is invoked when the image is successfully loaded. (A fourth parameter is also accepted for an error callback function.) We've seen all the rest of this code before except the `overdraw` option, which eliminates small gaps between the mesh's faces that arise due to limitations of the canvas API. (The `WebGLRenderer` does not need this property; it can align faces more perfectly.) You can see the result in the following screenshot:

Earth as a sphere with a mapped texture

The image used in this example is available in the Three.js package at `examples/textures/planets/land_ocean_ice_cloud_2048.jpg`.

There are a number of other options for different kinds of materials that are too complex to address in the space we have. You can read more about them in the documentation for the different materials. For example, the `MeshPhongMaterial` documentation (`http://threejs.org/docs/#Reference/Materials/MeshPhongMaterial`) includes notes on producing reflective surfaces.

A city scene

We've covered a lot of ground with the Three.js API. Let's tie it all together with a project that uses what we've learned about geometry and materials.

So far, we've been working with a single object in our world. If we wanted to move it around, we'd have to change its `position` vector. We could create a full scene this way by adding multiple objects and manually positioning them. However, for worlds with more than a few objects, this can quickly get quite tedious. There are several alternatives:

- **Rectangular layout**: This method involves storing a map in some simple format such as a string or an image, where each character or pixel color represents a type of object

- **Procedural generation**: This method involves the use of an algorithm to position objects semi-randomly

- **Editor**: This method involves the use of an external tool to construct the scene, followed by exporting the result (for example, in JSON format), and importing it when the application executes

The rectangular format is the easiest for simple game levels, and we'll be using it in *Chapter 3, Exploring and Interacting*. *Chapter 5, Design and Development* discusses the editor approach in detail. For now, let's try procedurally creating a city, based on an example created by *Ricardo Cabello* (the original Three.js author) at `http://www.mrdoob.com/lab/javascript/webgl/city/01/`.

First, let's create a cube and material that we'll use as the basis for our city buildings. We'll copy our geometry and material for each new building and scale the geometry appropriately:

```
var geo = new THREE.CubeGeometry(1, 1, 1);
geo.applyMatrix(new THREE.Matrix4().makeTranslation(0, 0.5, 0));
var material = new THREE.MeshDepthMaterial({overdraw: true});
```

The second line from the previous code snippet moves the geometry's origin (the point around which the geometry is scaled and rotated) to the bottom so that when we scale up a building, all the buildings' floors will be at the same height. This is done by shifting the y coordinate of every vertex and face 0.5 units up using a matrix that represents a vertical translation.

Matrices can be thought of as rectangular arrays or tables with rows and columns. A matrix with four rows and four columns is particularly useful for storing information about objects in 3D space because a single 4 x 4 matrix can represent position, rotation, and scale. This is the only point in this book that will mention matrices, so it's okay if you don't understand the underlying math; one of the reasons to use Three.js is to avoid having to do linear algebra manually. The transformation we are doing in this case is just one short way to move all the vertices and faces of a geometry at once without moving its origin.

Next, we'll create all our buildings:

```
for (var i = 0; i < 300; i++) {
  var building = new THREE.Mesh(geo.clone(), material.clone());
  building.position.x = Math.floor(Math.random() * 200 - 100) * 4;
  building.position.z = Math.floor(Math.random() * 200 - 100) * 4;
  building.scale.x = Math.random() * 50 + 10;
  building.scale.y = Math.random() * building.scale.x * 8 + 8;
  building.scale.z = building.scale.x;
  scene.add(building);
}
```

The only thing that's new here is the `clone()` method. Almost all Three.js objects can be cloned to create a copy that can be modified without altering the original. We are taking advantage of that to create new geometry and material instances based on our original instances.

Let's position the camera in a place where it can get a better view:

```
camera.position.y = 400;
camera.position.z = 400;
camera.rotation.x = -45 * Math.PI / 180;
```

We've seen rotation a couple of times now, but it's important to recall that rotation is measured in radians. The conversion we perform here tilts the camera 45 degrees down. You can also use the convenient `lookAt` method. For example, `camera.lookAt(new THREE.Vector3(0, 0, 0))` turns the camera to look at the default scene origin.

Finally, we'll add a floor as well:

```
var geo = new THREE.PlaneGeometry(2000, 2000, 20, 20);
var mat = new THREE.MeshBasicMaterial({color: 0x9db3b5, overdraw:
true});
var mesh = new THREE.Mesh(geo, mat);
mesh.rotation.x = -90 * Math.PI / 180;
scene.add(mesh);
```

The last two parameters to `PlaneGeometry()` split the plane into a 20 x 20 grid. This prevents Three.js from optimizing away the floor if it thinks all the vertices are too far out of view. Also, the plane is created along the x and y axes initially, so we need to rotate it by -90 degrees to make it lie flat under the buildings.

Putting it all together now:

```
var camera, scene, renderer;

function setup() {
  document.body.style.backgroundColor = '#d7f0f7';
  setupThreeJS();
  setupWorld();

  requestAnimationFrame(function animate() {
    renderer.render(scene, camera);
    requestAnimationFrame(animate);
  });
}

function setupThreeJS() {
  scene = new THREE.Scene();

  camera = new THREE.PerspectiveCamera(75, window.innerWidth /
  window.innerHeight, 1, 10000);
  camera.position.y = 400;
  camera.position.z = 400;
  camera.rotation.x = -45 * Math.PI / 180;

  renderer = new THREE.CanvasRenderer();
  renderer.setSize(window.innerWidth, window.innerHeight);
  document.body.appendChild(renderer.domElement);
}

function setupWorld() {
  // Floor
  var geo = new THREE.PlaneGeometry(2000, 2000, 20, 20);
  var mat = new THREE.MeshBasicMaterial({color: 0x9db3b5, overdraw:
  true});
  var floor = new THREE.Mesh(geo, mat);
```

```
floor.rotation.x = -90 * Math.PI / 180;
scene.add(floor);

// Original building
var geometry = new THREE.CubeGeometry(1, 1, 1);
geometry.applyMatrix(new THREE.Matrix4().makeTranslation(0, 0.5,
0));
var material = new THREE.MeshDepthMaterial({overdraw: true});

// Cloned buildings
for (var i = 0; i < 300; i++) {
  var building = new THREE.Mesh(geometry.clone(), material.clone());
  building.position.x = Math.floor(Math.random() * 200 - 100) * 4;
  building.position.z = Math.floor(Math.random() * 200 - 100) * 4;
  building.scale.x  = Math.random() * 50 + 10;
  building.scale.y  = Math.random() * building.scale.x * 8 + 8;
  building.scale.z  = building.scale.x;
  scene.add(building);
  }
}

// Run it!
setup();
```

Let's see the result, shown in the next screenshot:

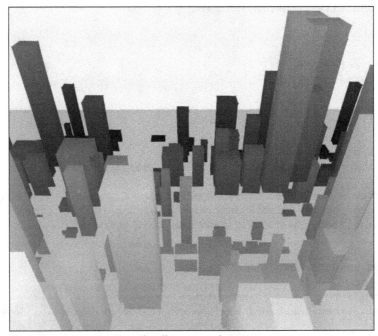

Procedurally generated cityscape

Let's optimize the scene by merging the geometries of all the buildings. To do this, we'll tweak the code that spawns our many buildings:

```
var cityGeometry = new THREE.Geometry();
for (var i = 0; i < 300; i++) {
  var building = new THREE.Mesh(geometry.clone());
  building.position.x = Math.floor(Math.random() * 200 - 100) * 4;
  building.position.z = Math.floor(Math.random() * 200 - 100) * 4;
  building.scale.x  = Math.random() * 50 + 10;
  building.scale.y  = Math.random() * building.scale.x * 8 + 8;
  building.scale.z  = building.scale.x;
  THREE.GeometryUtils.merge(cityGeometry, building);
}
var city = new THREE.Mesh(cityGeometry, material);
scene.add(city);
```

The key here is that we're now merging all of the building meshes into a single `cityGeometry` using `GeometryUtils.merge()`. This is an important optimization for scenes with a lot of geometry that does not move independently because the renderer can more intelligently batch drawing calls if it knows about all the vertices and faces at once instead of drawing them one mesh at a time.

Lighting

Lights are instances of `THREE.Light` that affect how the `MeshLambertMaterial` and `MeshPhongMaterial` surfaces are illuminated. Most lights have color (specified in hexadecimal notation like CSS colors) and intensity (a decimal value, usually between zero and one, indicating how bright the light should be). There are different kinds of lights as shown in the following table:

Type	Constructor	Description
Ambient	`THREE.AmbientLight(color)`	It affects all lit objects in the scene equally.
Directional	`THREE.DirectionalLight(color, intensity = 1)`	For this type, all light is parallel and comes from a given direction, as if the source was very far away.
Hemisphere	`THREE.HemisphereLight(skyColor, groundColor, intensity = 1)`	It simulates refractive lighting from the sun, sort of like two opposing directional lights.
Point	`THREE.PointLight(color, intensity = 1, radius = 0)`	It emanates from a specific point in space, like a lightbulb. It illuminates only objects within `radius`.

Type	Constructor	Description
Spot	`THREE.SpotLight(color, intensity, radius = 0, coneAngle = Math.PI / 3, falloff = 10)`	It emanates from a specific point in space in a specific direction. It illuminates objects in a cone pointing in its direction of rotation, falling off exponentially within a distance of `radius`.

To update our procedural city scene with lighting, let's first change the buildings' material to respond to light:

```
var material = new THREE.MeshPhongMaterial({overdraw: true, color:
0xcccccc});
```

Then we'll add our light to the scene:

```
var light = new THREE.DirectionalLight(0xf6e86d, 1);
light.position.set(1, 3, 2);
scene.add(light);
```

For directional lights, the direction of the light is the direction from `light.position` to `light.target.position`; both are vectors that you can change, and the target defaults to the world's origin.

Let's also change our renderer to WebGL because `CanvasRenderer` does not support advanced lighting features such as shadows and fog, which we'll want to add momentarily:

```
renderer = new THREE.WebGLRenderer();
```

As a final touch now that our scene has lighting, let's add fog for a little ambiance:

```
scene.fog = new THREE.FogExp2(0x9db3b5, 0.002);
```

There are actually two kinds of fog. `FoxExp2` gets exponentially denser with distance, and appropriately its parameters are color and density exponent (a small decimal you will need to play around with depending on the scale of your world). The other kind of fog is `THREE.Fog`, which gets denser linearly; its parameters are color, minimum distance at which fog starts appearing, and maximum distance beyond which objects will be occluded by fog. For example:

```
scene.fog = new THREE.Fog(0x9db3b5, 0, 800);
```

The differences between the two kinds of fog are difficult to capture in static images, but the next two screenshots show a contrast between exponential falloff and rapid linear falloff. The following screenshot shows `FogExp2` with low density:

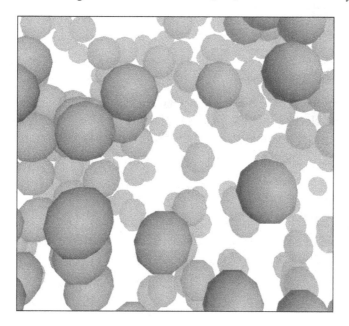

The following screenshot shows `Fog` with short falloff:

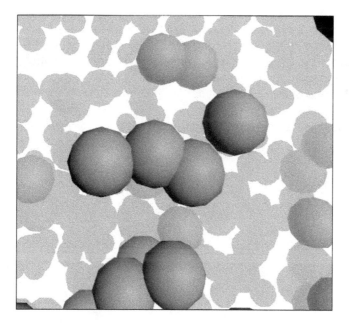

Shadows

Only the `DirectionalLight` and `PointLight` objects can cast shadows. Casting shadows first requires that we enable shadows on the renderer:

```
renderer.shadowMapEnabled = true;
```

If you want, you can also set `renderer.shadowMapSoft = true`, which will somewhat smooth the edges of the shadows.

Then, each object that will cast or receive shadows must be explicitly set to do so. (Shadows are disabled by default because calculating shadows can be slow.) For our city scene, we'll enable shadow receiving for our floor and both casting and receiving for our buildings:

```
floor.receiveShadow = true;
city.castShadow = true;
city.receiveShadow = true;
```

The `castShadow` and `receiveShadow` properties do pretty much what they sound like—enabling casting and receiving shadows.

Finally, we configure our `DirectionalLight` object to use shadows:

```
light.castShadow = true;
light.shadowDarkness = 0.5;
light.shadowMapWidth = 2048;
light.shadowMapHeight = 2048;
light.position.set(500, 1500, 1000);
light.shadowCameraFar = 2500;
// DirectionalLight only; not necessary for PointLight
light.shadowCameraLeft = -1000;
light.shadowCameraRight = 1000;
light.shadowCameraTop = 1000;
light.shadowCameraBottom = -1000;
```

We set the light to cast a shadow and set how dark we want it to be. The darkness usually ranges from 0 (no shadows) to 1 (dark shadows), but it can have other values; values below 0 will cause a sort of anti-shadow, where objects that would be in shadow are instead illuminated, and values higher than 1 will make shadows appear very black. Then we set the resolution of our shadows with the shadowMapWidth and shadowMapHeight properties, which affect the crispness of shadows' edges; higher values look sharper but are more computationally expensive. Next, we describe the **shadow camera** that will be used to project the shadows. In fact, when it comes to shadows, the DirectionalLight and PointLight objects are analogous to the OrthographicCamera and PerspectiveCamera objects in that the former uses parallel projection while the latter uses perspective projection. Therefore, to set up our camera, we move the light to a point that is far enough away to be able to *see* everything we want to have a shadow. Then we describe the shape of the frustum with the shadowCamera properties; the left, right, top, or bottom values are the lengths of the corresponding sides of the end of the frustum, and the Far value is the distance to the end of the frustum. (Recall from *Chapter 1, Hello, Three.js,* that a frustum is a shape encompassing what a camera can *see*.) If this is difficult to visualize, you can display the frustum like this:

```
light.shadowCameraVisible = true;
```

The result is a wireframe shape representing the shadow projection, shown in the next screenshot:

A shadow camera

The `DirectionalLight` object is positioned at the peak of the red cone, the ends of the yellow boxes are at the `shadowCameraNear` and `shadowCameraFar` distances, and the edges of the box are the size of the frustum. For `PointLights`, the entire frustum is a cone.

Renderers

Earlier, we switched from `CanvasRenderer` to `WebGLRenderer` in order to support shadows and fog. As a rule of thumb, `WebGLRenderer` is faster and has the most features, while `CanvasRenderer` has fewer features but broader browser support. One particularly nice feature of `WebGLRenderer` is that it supports antialiasing to smooth out jagged edges. We can enable this for our cityscape by passing the option in to the renderer constructor:

```
renderer = new THREE.WebGLRenderer({antialias: true});
```

With that, our cityscape is finally complete, as shown in the next screenshot:

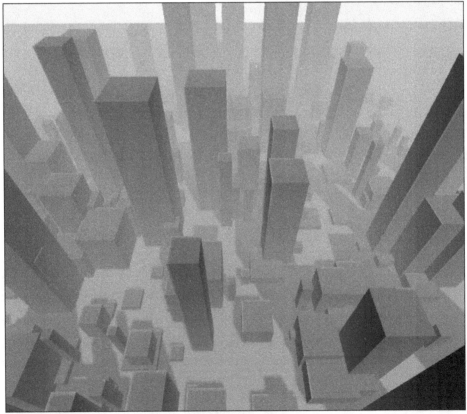

A completed city

Three.js has several other renderers, most notably for CSS and SVG. These can be found in the examples/js/renderers folder and are available as THREE.CSS3DRenderer and THREE.SVGRenderer, respectively, if their eponymous files are included in your HTML document. These renderers have a smaller set of supported features and are not as widely used, so they are not included in the main library, but they can be useful for scenes with a limited amount of primitive geometry and no lighting.

For the rest of this book, we'll be using the WebGLRenderer, so if you're using a version before version 11 of Internet Explorer, you should switch to Chrome or Firefox.

> If WebGL isn't available, your game can fall back to the CanvasRenderer or just display an error message. The easiest way to do this is with the script at examples/js/Detector.js. Once the script is included on your page, you can simply check the Detector.webgl Boolean to see if WebGL is supported on the current system. If it's not, you can call Detector.addGetWebGLMessage() to explain to the user why your game won't run on their device and how to switch to a browser that supports WebGL.

Summary

In this chapter, we learned how to work with different kinds of geometry, materials, and lighting. We also learned about renderers and scenes, and completed a project to build a city procedurally. In the next chapter, we'll learn about ways that users can interact with Three.js, add some physics to the mix, and build a basic first-person shooter game.

3
Exploring and Interacting

This chapter explains how users can interact with our games. We'll also cover some physics and use what we've learned to create a basic first-person shooter game.

Keyboard movement and mouse looking

In order to move our camera around, we're going to encapsulate some state, so let's define a `KeyboardControls` class in a new JavaScript file:

```
function KeyboardControls(object, options) {
  this.object = object;
  options = options || {};
  this.domElement = options.domElement || document;
  this.moveSpeed = options.moveSpeed || 1;

  this.domElement.addEventListener('keydown', this.onKeyDown.
  bind(this), false);
  this.domElement.addEventListener('keyup', this.onKeyUp.bind(this),
  false);
}

KeyboardControls.prototype = {
  update: function() {
    if (this.moveForward)  this.object.translateZ(-this.moveSpeed);
    if (this.moveBackward) this.object.translateZ( this.moveSpeed);
    if (this.moveLeft)     this.object.translateX(-this.moveSpeed);
    if (this.moveRight)    this.object.translateX( this.moveSpeed);
  },
  onKeyDown: function (event) {
    switch (event.keyCode) {
      case 38: /*up*/
```

```
        case 87: /*W*/ this.moveForward = true; break;

        case 37: /*left*/
        case 65: /*A*/ this.moveLeft = true; break;

        case 40: /*down*/
        case 83: /*S*/ this.moveBackward = true; break;

        case 39: /*right*/
        case 68: /*D*/ this.moveRight = true; break;
      }
    },
  onKeyUp: function (event) {
    switch(event.keyCode) {
      case 38: /*up*/
      case 87: /*W*/ this.moveForward = false; break;

      case 37: /*left*/
      case 65: /*A*/ this.moveLeft = false; break;

      case 40: /*down*/
      case 83: /*S*/ this.moveBackward = false; break;

      case 39: /*right*/
      case 68: /*D*/ this.moveRight = false; break;
      }
    }
  };
```

In the constructor, we added listeners for the `keydown` event and the `keyup` event so that when a key is pressed, we can keep track of the direction in which we should move. (In JavaScript, pressed keys are identified by numeric key codes.) In our `update` method, we just move in the specified direction. This is accomplished by checking flags that we set during key events so that we can poll the keyboard state during each frame. We can then use the controller by declaring it with `new KeyboardControls(camera)` and make it affect the camera in every frame by calling `controls.update(delta)` in our animation loop.

If you've ever written event-driven JavaScript before, most of this should look pretty familiar, and it's not hard to see how this could be extended in different ways to support different control mechanisms. Luckily, most applications are controlled pretty similarly, so Three.js provides a number of default control handlers that take care of most of this for you. These controllers are located in `examples/js/controls` and not in the main library, so you need to make sure to include them separately in your HTML file if you want to use them. Feel free to copy and extend an existing controller if you want a slightly different behavior, rather than writing your own controller from scratch every time.

The available controllers are:

Constructor	Important properties	Explanation

`FirstPersonControls`	`movementSpeed = 1.0`
	
	`lookSpeed = 0.005`
	
	`constrainVertical = false`
	
	`freeze = false`
		Keyboard movement (*WASD* or arrow keys for forward/back/strafe; up/down with *R* or *F*) and look around by following the mouse.

`FlyControls`	`movementSpeed = 1.0`
	
	`rollSpeed = 0.005`
		Press keys to move (*WASD*), tilt (*QE*), and look around (up/down/left/right).

`OculusControls`	`freeze = false`	Use the Oculus Rift virtual reality headset.

`OrbitControls`	`enabled = true`
	
	`target = new THREE.Vector3()`
	
	`zoomSpeed = 1.0`
	
	`minDistance = 0`
	
	`maxDistance = Infinity`
	
	`rotateSpeed = 1.0`
	
	`keyPanSpeed = 7.0`
	
	`autoRotateSpeed = 2.0`
		Rotate, pan, and zoom with mouse or touch controls, maintaining the *up* direction along the positive y axis.

Constructor	Important properties	Explanation
PathControls	duration = 10000 waypoints = [] lookSpeed = 0.005 lookVertical = true lookHorizontal = true	Move along a predefined route and look around by following the mouse.
PointerLockControls		Keyboard movement (*WASD* or arrow keys for forward/ back/strafe/jump) and look around by locking to the mouse. Requires that the canvas is in pointer lock mode.
TrackballControls	enabled = true rotateSpeed = 1.0 zoomSpeed = 1.2 panSpeed = 0.3 minDistance = 0 maxDistance = Infinity	Rotate, pan, zoom, and tilt with mouse or touch controls.
TransformControls	size = 1	Creates a widget around an object that allows users to rotate, scale, and translate it. Mainly used in an editor.

All the `controller` constructors take `camera` as their first parameter.

Let's add the `FirstPersonControls` controller to our city example from the last chapter and try flying around to see the city from the streets. First, we need to add the JavaScript file:

```
<script src="FirstPersonControls.js"></script>
```

Then, we'll add some globals:

```
var controls, clock;
```

Next, we'll instantiate the `controls` variable and the `clock` variable in `setupThreeJS()`:

```
clock = new THREE.Clock();
controls = new THREE.FirstPersonControls(camera);
controls.movementSpeed = 100;
controls.lookSpeed = 0.1;
```

A `clock` is a timer. We'll use it in this case to keep track of the amount of time that passes between each frame we draw. Also note that we changed the speed at which the camera moves and looks; otherwise, it feels very sluggish.

Finally, we'll change our animation loop in the `setup()` function to update our controller:

```
requestAnimationFrame(function animate() {
  renderer.render(scene, camera);
  controls.update(clock.getDelta());
  requestAnimationFrame(animate);
});
```

Updating the controls allows the camera to move when each frame is rendered. The clock's `getDelta` method returns the amount of time in seconds since the last time the `getDelta` method was called, so in this case it returns the number of seconds since the last frame was rendered. Internally, the controls use that delta to make sure that the animation is smooth over time. Now we can fly around our city!

You can see in the following screenshot what the city might look like from the ground:

Flying around the city

Clicking

Clicking on the screen in order to select or interact with something is a common requirement, but it's somewhat harder than it sounds because of the need to project the location of the click in the 2D plane of your screen into the 3D world of Three.js. To do this, we draw an imaginary line, called a ray, from the camera toward the position where the mouse might be in 3D space and see if it intersects with anything.

In order to project, we first need a projector:

```
projector = new THREE.Projector();
```

Then we need to register a listener on the click event for the canvas:

```
renderer.domElement.addEventListener('mousedown', function(event) {
  var vector = new THREE.Vector3(
      renderer.devicePixelRatio * (event.pageX - this.offsetLeft) /
      this.width * 2 - 1,
     -renderer.devicePixelRatio * (event.pageY - this.offsetTop) /
      this.height * 2 + 1,
    0
    );
  projector.unprojectVector(vector, camera);

  var raycaster = new THREE.Raycaster(
    camera.position,
    vector.sub(camera.position).normalize()
  );
  var intersects = raycaster.intersectObjects(OBJECTS);
  if (intersects.length) {
    // intersects[0] describes the clicked object
  }
}, false);
```

> The previous code assumes that you are using the `PerspectiveCamera` class. If you are using the `OrthographicCamera` class, projectors have a utility method that returns an appropriate raycaster, and you do not have to un-project the vector first:
>
> ```
> var raycaster = projector.pickingRay(vector, camera);
> ```

The previous code listens to the mousedown event on the renderer's canvas. Then, it creates a new Vector3 instance with the mouse's coordinates on the screen relative to the center of the canvas as a percent of the canvas width. That vector is then un-projected (from 2D into 3D space) relative to the camera.

Once we have the point in 3D space representing the mouse's location, we draw a line to it using the Raycaster. The two arguments that it receives are the starting point and the direction to the ending point. We determine the direction by subtracting the mouse and camera positions and then normalizing the result, which divides each dimension by the length of the vector to scale it so that no dimension has a value greater than 1. Finally, we use the ray to check which objects are located in the given direction (that is, under the mouse) with the intersectObjects method. OBJECTS is an array of objects (generally meshes) to check; be sure to change it appropriately for your code. An array of objects that are behind the mouse are returned and sorted by distance, so the first result is the object that was clicked.

Each object in the intersects array has an object, point, face, and distance property. Respectively, the values of these properties are the clicked object (generally a Mesh), a Vector3 instance representing the clicked location in space, the Face3 instance at the clicked location, and the distance from the camera to the clicked point.

It's also possible to go in reverse (3D to 2D) by projecting instead of un-projecting:

```
var widthHalf  = 0.5 * renderer.domElement.width  / renderer.
devicePixelRatio,
  heightHalf = 0.5 * renderer.domElement.height / renderer.
  devicePixelRatio;

var vector = mesh.position.clone(); // or an arbitrary point
projector.projectVector(vector, camera);

vector.x =  vector.x * widthHalf  + widthHalf;
vector.y = -vector.y * heightHalf + heightHalf;
```

After this code runs, vector.x and vector.y will hold the horizontal and vertical coordinates of the specified point relative to the upper-left corner of the canvas. (Make sure you actually specify the point you want, instead of using mesh.position.clone(), and that you've instantiated your projector.) Note that the resulting coordinates might not be over the canvas if the original 3D point is not on the screen.

The last thing you want when your player is clicking madly to shoot at enemies is for the whole screen to suddenly turn blue because the browser thinks the user is trying to select something. To avoid this, you can either cancel the `select` event in JavaScript with `document.onselectstart = function() { return false; }` or disable it in CSS:

```css
* {
    -webkit-user-select: none;
    -moz-user-select: none;
    -ms-user-select: none;
    user-select: none;
}
```

Timing

As we start building more realistic examples, you'll notice delta parameters being passed around to functions that affect physics. Those deltas represent an amount of time since the last time physics was calculated, and they're used to smooth out movement over time.

The naive way to move objects in code is to simply change the object's position. For example, to move an object across the canvas, you might write `obj.x += 10` inside your animation loop to move it 10 units every frame. This approach suffers from the issue that it is dependent on the frame rate. In other words, if your game is running slowly (that is, fewer frames per second), your object will also appear to move slowly, whereas if your game is running quickly (that is, more frames per second), your object will appear to move quickly.

One solution is to multiply the speed by the amount of time that has passed between rendering frames. For example, if you want your object to move 600 units per second, you might write `obj.x += 600 * delta`. In this way, your object will move a constant distance over time. However, at low frame rates and high speeds, your object will be moving large distances every frame, which can cause it to do strange things such as move through walls. At high frame rates, computing your physics might take longer than the amount of time between frames, which will cause your application to freeze and crash (this is called a *spiral of death*). Additionally, we would like to achieve perfect reproducibility. That is, every time we run the application with the same input, we would like exactly the same output. If we have variable frame deltas, our output will diverge the longer the program runs due to accumulated rounding errors, even at normal frame rates.

A better solution is to separate physics update time-steps from frame refresh time-steps. The physics engine should receive fixed-size time deltas, while the rendering engine should determine how many physics updates should occur per frame. The fixed-size deltas avoid an inconsistent rounding error and ensure that there are no giant leaps between frames. The following code shows how to divide the amount of time between frames into discrete chunks to use for physics calculations:

```
// Globals
INV_MAX_FPS = 1 / 60;
frameDelta = 0;
clock = new THREE.Clock();

// In the animation loop (the requestAnimationFrame callback)…
frameDelta += clock.getDelta();
while (frameDelta >= INV_MAX_FPS) {
  update(INV_MAX_FPS); // calculate physics
  frameDelta -= INV_MAX_FPS;
}
```

First, we declare INV_MAX_FPS, the multiplicative inverse of the maximum frames per second that we want to render (60 in this case). This is the time-step we will feed to our physics engine via the update function, and you may need to adjust it depending on how slowly your simulation runs (keep in mind that most monitors can't refresh faster than 60 frames per second, and above 30 is usually considered acceptable). Then, we start tracking our frameDelta, the accumulated amount of time since the last physics update. Our clock will be used to keep track of the time between rendering frames.

In the animation loop, we first add the amount of time since the last render to frameDelta, then perform as many fixed-size physics updates as we need. We might end up with some time left over in frameDelta, but it will be used up during the next frame.

For our purposes, "physics updates" means both moving objects in our world and moving the player's camera.

First-person shooter project

Let's write a real game! This project will be bigger than any others we've done, so let's start by specifying exactly what to accomplish. We're going to build an arena-based first-person shooter game with the following features:

- A world based on a voxel map
- A player that can look, run, and jump around in the world

- Pointer lock and full-screen, so that the player is fully immersed as in a desktop or console game
- The player should be able to shoot at enemies that wander around, and the enemies should shoot back
- The player's and enemies' health should deteriorate when shot, and players should respawn when they run out of health
- The player's screen should flash red when shot
- There should be a **HUD (heads-up display)** with crosshairs and a health indicator
- We do not care much about lighting or texturing, except that the player must be able to see and perceive distances in depth

 The complete code is too long to include here, but you can download it online from your account at http://www.packtpub.com or have the files e-mailed to you at http://www.packtpub.com/support. The rest of this section covers interesting excerpts from the code.

The first step is to write the HTML code. In the previous examples, we've written all of our code in a single HTML file, but this is a bigger project so we should split the code into separate files and reference them from our index.html file. We'll also want to add some user-interface elements to the basic HTML document, notably including a start screen that the user must click in order to enter the game and a hurt div, which is just a translucent red overlay that we'll flash briefly on the screen as a helpful warning when the player gets hit by an enemy bullet.

```
<html>
  <head>
    <!-- ... -->
    <link rel="stylesheet" href="main.css" />
  </head>
  <body>
    <div id="start"><div id="instructions">
      Click to start
    </div></div>
    <div id="hud" class="hidden">
      <!-- ... -->
      <div id="hurt" class="hidden"></div>
    </div>
    <script src="three.min.js"></script>
    <script src="main.js"></script>
  </body>
</html>
```

We'll also break up the `main.js` file into a few different files when we start writing classes. For simplicity we've put everything in the same folder. In *Chapter 5, Design and Development*, we take a closer look at better organizational structures for large projects.

Designing a map

Now that we have a place to put some code, we need an interesting world to look at. Let's design a map to use. For example:

```
var map = "XXXXXXX  \n" +
          "X      X \n" +
          "X  S   X \n" +
          "X      X \n" +
          "X    S XXX\n" +
          "XXX      X\n" +
          "  XX  S X\n" +
          "   X    X\n" +
          "    XXXXXX";
map = map.split("\n");
var HORIZONTAL_UNIT = 100,
    VERTICAL_UNIT   = 100,
    ZSIZE = map.length * HORIZONTAL_UNIT,
    XSIZE = map[0].length * HORIZONTAL_UNIT;
```

Our map is represented as a string where x indicates a wall and s indicates a location where players can spawn into the world. We split the string into an array for easier access, then decide how big each voxel should be (in this case, 100 * 100 * 100 as indicated by the HORIZONTAL_UNIT and VERTICAL_UNIT variables) and track how big the map is overall using XSIZE and ZSIZE.

Next, we need to use our map to generate the 3D world:

```
for (var i = 0, rows = map.length; i < rows; i++) {
  for (var j = 0, cols = map[i].length; j < cols; j++) {
    addVoxel(map[i].charAt(j), i, j);
  }
}
```

This is pretty straightforward—iterating over the map and adding something into the world at the specified row and column. Our addVoxel method looks similar to the following code:

```
function addVoxel(type, row, col) {
  var z = (row+1) * HORIZONTAL_UNIT - ZSIZE * 0.5,
```

```
          x = (col+1) * HORIZONTAL_UNIT - XSIZE * 0.5;
    switch(type) {
      case ' ': break;
      case 'S':
        spawnPoints.push(new THREE.Vector3(x, 0, z));
        break;
      case 'X':
        var geo = new THREE.CubeGeometry(HORIZONTAL_UNIT,
        VERTICAL_UNIT, HORIZONTAL_UNIT);
        var material = new THREE.MeshPhongMaterial({
          color: Math.random() * 0xffffff
        });
        var mesh = new THREE.Mesh(geo, material);
        mesh.position.set(x, VERTICAL_UNIT*0.5, z);
        scene.add(mesh);
        break;
    }
  }
```

In order to see our world, we'll also need to add lighting (the easiest approach is one or two DirectionalLights similar to what we used in the city project) and you may also want to add fog to help with depth perception. You can manually adjust the camera's position and rotation to see what you've just constructed, or temporarily add FirstPersonControls similar to what we used in the city project. Since we are only using our map to add walls, you should add a floor as we did in the city project as well, using a single large plane.

Constructing a player

Now that we have a world, let's create a player that can move around in it. We'll need a Player class to keep track of each player's state, so let's extend THREE.Mesh in a new file, which we'll call player.js:

```
function Player() {
  THREE.Mesh.apply(this, arguments);
  this.rotation.order = 'YXZ';
  this._aggregateRotation = new THREE.Vector3();
  this.cameraHeight = 40;
  this.velocity = new THREE.Vector3();
  this.acceleration = new THREE.Vector3(0, -150, 0);
  this.ambientFriction = new THREE.Vector3(-10, 0, -10);
  this.moveDirection = {
    FORWARD: false,
    BACKWARD: false,
```

```
      LEFT: false,
      RIGHT: false
    };
  }
  Player.prototype = Object.create(THREE.Mesh.prototype);
  Player.prototype.constructor = Player;
```

We implemented `Player` as a child of the `THREE.Mesh` class by calling the `Mesh` constructor from inside the `Player` constructor and copying over the `prototype`. This means that players automatically have geometry, materials, position, rotation, and scaling, and additionally we can implement our own features (such as velocity and acceleration). Note that the player functions similar to a controller because it contains code to move and look around, with the difference that the input event handlers are bound outside the class in order to make it reusable.

One thing that may look strange here is changing the `rotation.order`. Rotation is tracked using a Euler representation, which consists of angles in radians around each axis in addition to the order in which the axial rotation should be applied. The default order is `'XYZ'`, which rotates up and down first (x), then left to right (y). In this configuration, the world will appear to tilt if the player looks horizontally after looking vertically. To visualize this, imagine tilting a donut so that the side away from you is up and the side near you is down; that is x rotation, or **pitch**. If you then move your finger around the donut from the front to the left, that is y rotation, or **yaw**. (Tilting the donut to the right would be z rotation, or **roll**.) Notice that if you were looking out from the middle of the donut towards your finger, your head would be tilted relative to the world. As a result, we have to change the Euler order to `'YXZ'` to make the camera rotate relative to the world instead of to itself. With this change, we move our finger first, then tilt the donut so our finger goes up or down instead of the front of the donut, and we end up with a level head.

To actually implement this looking around, we'll lock the mouse and track its movement. We'll use libraries to make this easier since the APIs are a little wordy. You can get `PointerLock.js` at `https://github.com/IceCreamYou/PointerLock.js` and BigScreen from *Brad Dougherty* at `https://github.com/bdougherty/BigScreen`. Once we have included these libraries, starting the game looks similar to the following code, which requests the browser to enter full screen and pointer lock mode before starting animation:

```
document.getElementById('start').addEventListener('click', function()
{
  if (BigScreen.enabled) {
    var instructions = this;
    BigScreen.request(document.body, function() {
      PL.requestPointerLock(document.body, function() {
        instructions.className = 'hidden';
```

```
          startAnimating();
        }, function() {
          stopAnimating();
        });
      }, function() {
        instructions.className = 'exited';
        stopAnimating();
      });
    }
  });
```

The Pointer Lock and Full Screen APIs can only be engaged when users take an action (clicking or hitting the keyboard) as a security precaution to prevent attackers from hijacking your screen, so we're waiting for a click in this case. Once we're in full screen, we can listen to the mousemove event to rotate the player:

```
document.addEventListener('mousemove', function(event) {
  player.rotate(event.movementY, event.movementX, 0);
}, false);
```

 The event.movementX property and the event.movementY property are normalized across browsers here by the PointerLock.js library.

The rotate() method simply changes the player's _aggregateRotation vector. We're assuming here that the player has been instantiated, as shown in the following code:

```
player = new Player();
player.add(camera);
scene.add(player);
```

Yes, we just added the camera to the player. It turns out that any object that is a descendant of THREE.Object3D can have other objects added to it. Those child objects are accessible through the parent's children array, and they will be grouped together with the parent so that movement, rotation, and scaling are composed. (In other words, if a child's local position is (0, 0, 5) and the parent's position is (0, 0, 10), then the child's position in the world will be (0, 0, 15). Rotation and scale work similarly.) In this case, we use this composition to cause our camera to follow our player around.

Because child objects' position, rotation, and scaling are relative to the parent's position, rotation, and scaling, you could create a third-person camera by positioning the camera on the positive z axis (and probably a little higher on the y axis) and giving the `player` object a geometry and material (remember, `Player` inherits from `Mesh`, so you can instantiate a player with `new Player(geometry, material)`).

Player movement

We'll finish off the code to look around in a moment, but because it's closely related to the player's movement, let's address that first.

Physical movement

Getting movement right is a complex topic. Although simply adding a constant velocity to an object's position can work for some simulations, more advanced games will want to have acceleration at play (for example, for gravity) and potentially other forces as well. The most straightforward approach to linear forces is to keep track of acceleration and velocity vectors and add them together:

```
// When the mesh is instantiated
mesh.velocity = new THREE.Vector3(0, 0, 0);
mesh.acceleration = new THREE.Vector3(0, 0, 0);

// Called in the animation loop
function update(delta) {
  // Apply acceleration
  mesh.velocity.add(mesh.acceleration().clone().
multiplyScalar(delta));
  // Apply velocity
  mesh.position.add(mesh.velocity.clone().multiplyScalar(delta));
}
```

This is called **Euler** integration (pronounced oiler, not yew-ler). A simple modification gives us **Midpoint** integration, which yields a reasonable improvement in accuracy. All we need to do is apply the acceleration in halves before and after applying velocity:

```
var halfAccel = mesh.acceleration.clone().multiplyScalar(delta *
0.5);
// Apply half acceleration (first half of midpoint formula)
mesh.velocity.add(halfAccel);
// Apply thrust
mesh.position.add(mesh.velocity.clone().multiplyScalar(delta));
// Apply half acceleration (second half of midpoint formula)
mesh.velocity.add(halfAccel);
```

To understand how this works, consider the following graph:

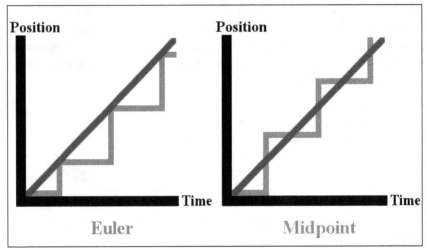

Euler versus Midpoint integration

The goal of our integration formula is to stay as close to the true position as possible. In the graph, the vertical jumps are at our time-steps, where physics updates are calculated. The midpoint curve is just a shift of the Euler curve so that the area between the midpoint and true positions cancel out. More error is introduced when acceleration, jerk, and nonlinear forces are applied, but for our purposes (and in the space we have) the midpoint formula is a reasonable trade-off between simplicity and accuracy.

The **fourth-order Runge-Kutta** method (also known as **RK4**) is another commonly used method for computing motion over time. RK4 extrapolates several intermediate states between frames, resulting in a more accurate final approximation for the state in the next frame. The trade-off for increased accuracy is increased complexity and decreased speed. Because of its complexity, we won't cover it here, but usually if you need something as sophisticated as this, you will want to delegate physics handling to one of the libraries addressed in the next section on collision.

Updating the player's movement and rotation

Let's listen for the movement keys so that we know when to move the player:

```
document.addEventListener('keydown', function(event) {
  switch (event.keyCode) {
    case 38: // up
    case 87: // w
      player.moveDirection.FORWARD = true;
      break;
    case 37: // left
    case 65: // a
      player.moveDirection.LEFT = true;
      break;
    case 40: // down
    case 83: // s
      player.moveDirection.BACKWARD = true;
      break;
    case 39: // right
    case 68: // d
      player.moveDirection.RIGHT = true;
      break;
    case 32: // space
      player.jump();
      break;
  }
}, false);
```

We'll check these flags in every frame to see how much thrust to apply. We also need a `keyup` listener, which looks almost identical to the `keydown` listener except that it should set our directions back to `false` when the relevant keys are released.

And now, finally, we can implement the player's `update` method:

```
Player.prototype.update = (function() {
  var halfAccel = new THREE.Vector3();
  var scaledVelocity = new THREE.Vector3();
  return function(delta) {
    var r = this._aggregateRotation
      .multiplyScalar(delta)
      .add(this.rotation);
    r.x = Math.max(Math.PI * -0.5, Math.min(Math.PI * 0.5, r.x));
    this.rotation.x = 0;

    if (this.moveDirection.FORWARD) this.velocity.z -= Player.SPEED;
    if (this.moveDirection.LEFT) this.velocity.x -= Player.SPEED;
    if (this.moveDirection.BACKWARD) this.velocity.z += Player.SPEED;
    if (this.moveDirection.RIGHT) this.velocity.x += Player.SPEED;

    halfAccel.copy(this.acceleration).multiplyScalar(delta * 0.5);
    this.velocity.add(halfAccel);
    var squaredVelocity = this.velocity.x*this.velocity.x +
    this.velocity.z*this.velocity.z;
    if (squaredVelocity > Player.SPEED*Player.SPEED) {
      var scalar = Player.SPEED / Math.sqrt(squaredVelocity);
      this.velocity.x *= scalar;
      this.velocity.z *= scalar;
    }
    scaledVelocity.copy(this.velocity).multiplyScalar(delta);
    this.translateX(scaledVelocity.x);
    this.translateZ(scaledVelocity.z);
    this.position.y += scaledVelocity.y;
    this.velocity.add(halfAccel);

    this.velocity.add(scaledVelocity.multiply(
      this.ambientFriction
    ));

    this.rotation.set(r.x, r.y, r.z);
    this._aggregateRotation.set(0, 0, 0);
  };
})();
```

There's a lot going on here. The first thing to notice is that our definition of the method immediately invokes an anonymous function that returns our actual method definition. We do this to create some helper objects for efficiency. Most Three.js math happens in place (as opposed to returning a new object with the result of each operation), which means that to perform calculations with existing math objects such as the `acceleration` vector, we either need to clone them or copy values to a `helper` object that we can manipulate without side effects. Cloning creates too much garbage-collection churn, meaning that the browser will lag if it has to process all the objects we would be rapidly creating and then discarding. Instead, we define the `halfAccel` vector, for example, in a closure (so that it doesn't pollute the global namespace) and do our vector math with that. This pattern is used frequently in the Three.js library itself.

Almost everything else in the `update` method is addition and multiplication. To look around, we aggregate how far the mouse has moved between each frame, then add the corresponding amount of rotation when the player is updating. Also, the acceleration and velocity part should look familiar — it's the same midpoint strategy we just covered in the *Physical movement* section. We have to be sensitive to a few issues though. First, we restrict `r.x` in order to constrain how far the player can look up and down so that they don't get confused which way is up. Second, we want the concept of *forward* to be relative to the world instead of where the camera is looking, so that we can look up and walk forward without flying into the air in the direction we're looking. To do this, we reset the pitch (making the player look straight ahead instead of up or down) before adding the velocity to the position. Finally, we add friction, which allows the player to slow down and stop after moving in a given direction. In your actual game, you will probably want to use different levels of friction depending on whether your player is in the air or not.

Player collision

There are several different approaches to detecting collision:

- **Voxels**: As discussed in *Chapter 2, Building a World*, one common way to design worlds is to use a string or image to represent repeatable building blocks, such as LEGOs. When using this method, the fastest way to check for collision between an actor and the world is to simply check if the actor's coordinates are inside the zone that the map designates for use by a building block. This avoids the complexity of comparing 3D shapes.

- **Rays**: Just like we used the `Raycaster` class earlier to detect clicked objects, we can also use it to detect collision between multiple objects with the `intersectObjects()` method. To do this, we can cast rays in multiple directions from the object that needs to check for collision, such as the player; for example, we could cast a ray from the player's position toward each of the player's vertices. If an intersection occurs at a distance smaller than the distance from the player's position to the vertex, a collision has occurred. There are several problems with this method. First, it's inefficient for large numbers of vertices or dynamic objects. Second, objects can escape detection if they are not exactly in the direction of a ray. Lastly, rays check for intersection using an approximation of objects' shapes, so irregularly-shaped objects can be incorrectly selected. However, this is the simplest general-purpose approach that can work without additional libraries or knowledge about the world's layout.

- **Intersection**: We can manually compare objects' geometries and positions to see if they overlap. Since detecting collision between complex 3D shapes is mathematically difficult, most games use simplified approximations instead of the actual geometry to make calculations easier. Even so, 3D collision detection algorithms are complex and slow unless we use very simple shapes such as boxes or spheres that don't do a great job of approximating our objects. It's also computationally expensive without some complex optimizations such as using a data structure called an **Octree** to make sure only nearby objects need to check for collision. If you want to try implementing your own collision, Three.js includes an Octree implementation in the `examples/js` folder.

- **Libraries**: Luckily, we don't have to do complex collision detection manually, as there are several libraries that can take care of the complications for us. They also handle collision response and associated physics. The leading contenders are:
    - **Ammo.js** is a large but complete library compiled to JavaScript from C++. It is available at `https://github.com/kripken/ammo.js/`.
    - **Cannon.js** is a smaller library written from scratch in JavaScript and inspired in part by concepts from Three.js. It is available at `https://github.com/schteppe/cannon.js`.
    - **Physi.js** is a bridge between Ammo or Cannon and Three.js that also runs the physics simulation in a separate thread to avoid blocking the rendering. It is available at `https://github.com/chandlerprall/Physijs`.

For our shooter game, we'll use voxel collision and a little bit of manual intersection. Unfortunately, all the physics libraries are large, so we don't have space to cover their APIs here. However, Cannon.js and Physi.js have examples specifically for use with Three.js available from their project pages.

Voxel collision

If we try to walk around our world now, we'll just fall through the floor. Let's create a function to check for collision between the player and the voxel world:

```
function checkPlayerCollision(player) {
  player.collideFloor(floor.position.y);
  var cell = mapCellFromPosition(player.position);
  switch (cell.char) {
    case ' ':
    case 'S':
      break;
    case 'X':
      moveOutside(cell, player);
      break;
  }
}
```

Our `collideFloor` method keeps the player above the floor's y position. Then, the `mapCellFromPosition` method looks up the map cell from the player's position to determine whether the player is in a wall or open space. If the player is colliding with a wall, the `moveOutside()` method moves the player outside of it by shifting the player toward the closest cell. The cell-from-position lookup is just the reverse of what we used to place each voxel originally:

```
var XOFFSET = (map.length+1) * 0.5 * HORIZONTAL_UNIT,
    ZOFFSET = (map[0].length+1) * 0.5 * HORIZONTAL_UNIT,
    col = Math.floor((position.x+XOFFSET) / HORIZONTAL_UNIT) - 1,
    row = Math.floor((position.z+ZOFFSET) / HORIZONTAL_UNIT) - 1,
    char = map[mapRow].charAt(mapCol);
```

Bots

Now that we've got the player working, it's time to add enemy bots. Enemies can be `Players` just as the user is, so apart from initializing them, the main thing we need to add is autonomous behavior. We don't have the space here to go in depth on artificial intelligence strategies, so we'll just set each bot's `moveDirection` flags randomly every once in awhile:

```
bot.rotation.y = Math.random() * Math.PI * 2;
bot.moveDirection.FORWARD = Math.random() < 0.8;
```

Bullets

Finally, let's add shooting so we can pulverize those enemies! First, we'll create a
new `Bullet` class in `bullet.js` similar to what we did for the `Player` class. Bullets
are just meshes with a `direction` vector and a `speed` scalar, so their `update` method
can be pretty simple:

```
Bullet.prototype.update = (function() {
  var scaledDirection = new THREE.Vector3();
  return function(delta) {
    scaledDirection.copy(this.direction).multiplyScalar(this.
    speed*delta);
    this.position.add(scaledDirection);
  };
})();
```

We'll set bullets' directions when they're shot. Bullets can either be shot in the
camera's direction or from an enemy bot toward another player. To get the
relevant direction, our `shoot` function will look similar to the following code:

```
var shoot = (function() {
  var negativeZ = new THREE.Vector3(0, 0, -1);
  return function(from, to) {
    bullet = new Bullet();
    bullet.position.copy(from.position);
    if (to) {
      bullet.direction = to.position.clone().sub(from.position).
      normalize();
    }
    else {
      bullet.direction = negativeZ.clone().applyEuler(from.rotation);
    }
    bullets.push(bullet);
    scene.add(bullet);
  };
})();
```

We get the direction from one player to another by subtracting their positions.
If the user is shooting then we aren't necessarily aiming at anything, so we just
want the direction in which the camera is looking. We retrieve this direction
from the player's rotation.

Updating the game loop

Bringing it all together, we should end up with a function like this, which executes all of our game's behavior:

```
function update(delta) {
  player.update(delta);
  checkPlayerCollision(player);

  for (var i = bullets.length - 1; i >= 0; i--) {
    bullets[i].update(delta);
    checkBulletCollision(bullets[i], i);
  }

  for (var j = 0; j < enemies.length; j++) {
    var enemy = enemies[j];
    enemy.update(delta);
    checkPlayerCollision(enemy);
    if (enemy.health <= 0) {
      spawn(enemy);
    }
    shoot(enemy, player);
    move(enemy);
  }

  if (player.health <= 0) {
    spawn(player);
  }
}
```

This function calculates all physics (including movement and collision checking), triggers autonomous behavior such as the bots shooting at targets, and implements game logic (such as players dying when their health is too low). It is called in every frame from the animation loop. The delta parameter is the physics time-step, so it should always be the same value as discussed in the *Timing* section of this chapter.

That was a lot of code to write! We're rewarded, though, with an awesome arena-based first-person shooter game that you can put online and send to all your friends. You can see how all that work might look in the following image:

A screenshot of the finished game

Summary

In this chapter, we learned how to implement user interaction and game physics. We also built a full-fledged first-person shooter game. In the next chapter, we'll add detail to our worlds with imported models, particle systems, sound, and post-processing effects.

4
Adding Detail

This chapter explains how to manage external assets such as 3D models, as well as add details to your worlds with particle systems, sound, and graphic effects. It will also elaborate on the arena first-person shooter game we built in *Chapter 3, Exploring and Interacting*, to turn it into a Capture-the-Flag game.

Setting up CTF

In order to have a proper Capture-the-Flag game, we first need to have teams. There are several things that need to be associated with a given team:

- Flags (and the flag color)
- Players (and the player skins)
- Spawn points
- Bullets (if you want to avoid same-team damage)
- Potentially map decorations/materials

The simplest way to associate each of these elements with a team is to just add a property with a simple value such as R or B to represent Red or Blue (or some other team name). A more advanced approach could be to create a Team class that holds references to everything that belongs to that team, since that could offer optimizations such as limiting the number of collision checks that need to be performed. If you do that, however, make sure you remove all the appropriate references from the Team container when removing something (such as a bullet) from the world in order to avoid memory leaks.

Next, we need to modify our map to add flags for the Red and Blue teams, which we'll represent as R and B, respectively:

```
var map = "XXXXXXX    \n" +
          "X   S   X    \n" +
          "X   R   X    \n" +
          "X      XX  \n" +
          "X       XXX\n" +
          "XXX       X\n" +
          "  XX       X\n" +
          "   X  B   X\n" +
          "   X  S   X\n" +
          "     XXXXXXX";
```

Now we need to actually add those flags to the world. Flags are not simple geometric primitive shapes though, so we'll want to import a more complex mesh.

Asset management

Primitive geometric shapes are great for tests, but any serious game these days will likely make heavy use of 3D models created in a specialized program such as Blender, Maya, or 3ds Max. These models need to be imported into Three.js scenes and converted to THREE.Mesh objects with geometry and materials. Luckily, Three.js provides importers called **loaders** for a variety of file formats.

Loaders

For our flags, we'll use a simple mesh in Collada format. (Collada is an XML-based format for storing 3D mesh and animation data, with files ending in .dae.) You can download our flag mesh from the Packt Publishing website. The ColladaLoader is not included in the main Three.js library, but can be copied from examples/js/loaders/ColladaLoader.js and then included in your HTML as:

```
<script src="ColladaLoader.js"></script>
```

Then the model can be loaded like this:

```
var loader = new THREE.ColladaLoader();
loader.load('flag.dae', function(result) {
  scene.add(result.scene);
});
```

Often imported models need to be resized and repositioned, so you will probably want to set `result.scene.scale` and `result.scene.position` before adding the mesh to the world. You can see the loaded model in the next screenshot:

The Blue team's flag

 By default, importing meshes will not work on local `file:///` URLs. This is because when JavaScript requests the file, browsers' default security settings refuse to return local system files. To get around this restriction, you can either run a local HTTP server or change your browser's security settings as described at `https://github.com/mrdoob/three.js/wiki/How-to-run-things-locally`.

There are many other loaders for models in other file formats, including CTM, OBJ, MTL, PLY, STL, UTF8, VRML, and VTK. These are located in the `examples/js/loaders` folder. Almost all of the loaders have a `load` method, like the `ColladaLoader` method mentioned previously, which takes a function to call when loading is finished. However, loaders do not have a standardized format, and some of them work in slightly different ways. In particular, the parameters passed to the callback depend on the file type. You should check the `examples` folder for demos of the loader you want to use to make sure you handle the returned result correctly.

In our case, we get a group of sub-meshes (in the `result.scene`) back from the `ColladaLoader` because Collada files can contain multiple meshes. We need to modify the flag's materials to make sure each flag reflects its team's color:

```
result.scene.children[1].material = new THREE.MeshLambertMaterial({
  color: type === 'R' ? 0xee1100 : 0x0066ee,
  side: THREE.DoubleSide,
});
```

Recall that when we set up our camera to follow the player around in the last chapter, we added the camera to the `player` object. Whenever objects are grouped together this way, they can be accessed through the parent's `children` array. In this case, we're using that array to alter the material for the cloth part of the flag to make it blue or red depending on which team it belongs to.

In addition to loaders for standard 3D model file formats, there are a number of Three.js-specific loaders included directly in the library. In particular, `THREE.JSONLoader` is designed to load single meshes, while `THREE.SceneLoader` can load entire scenes (including lighting, cameras, and other Three.js entities).

There are also built-in loaders for assets other than 3D models. For example, we've already seen `THREE.TextureLoader` at work behind the scenes of `THREE.ImageUtils.loadTexture`. You can also directly load pieces of meshes, including geometry, images, and materials. Other objects such as lights, cameras, and even arbitrary resources can be loaded as well. However, these loaders are normally invoked under the hood of the library rather than directly by developers because it usually makes more sense to load entire models or scenes rather than the individual pieces. As a result, we will not cover these loaders here, but you can find them in the `src/loaders` folder if you would like to learn more.

Like `ColladaLoader`, the `JSONLoader` uses a `load` method with a callback. However, the callback receives a `THREE.Geometry` object as its first parameter. Not all 3D models have associated materials, but if the object does have materials, they will be passed to the callback in an array as the second parameter:

```
var loader = new THREE.JSONLoader();
loader.load('model.js', function(geometry, materials) {
  var material = materials && materials.length ?
    new THREE.MeshFaceMaterial(materials) :
    new THREE.MeshBasicMaterial({ color: 0x000000 });
  var mesh = new THREE.Mesh(geometry, material);
  scene.add(mesh);
});
```

As explained in *Chapter 2, Building a World*, `MeshFaceMaterial` is a container that maps multiple materials to different faces of the mesh.

The `SceneLoader` is a little different from other loaders because it can use other loaders to handle specific parts of the scene:

```
var loader = new THREE.SceneLoader();
loader.addGeometryHandler('ctm', THREE.CTMLoader);
loader.addHierarchyHandler('dae', THREE.ColladaLoader);
loader.load('scene.js', function(result) {
scene.add(result.scene);
});
```

If a scene includes an external model, the `SceneLoader` will try to import it using the appropriate handler. Use the `addGeometryHandler` method to add loaders for file formats that only support single meshes, and use `addHierarchyHandler` to add loaders for file formats that support multimesh scenes (DAE, OBJ, and UTF8). In this example, CTM and DAE files will be loaded correctly.

Exporting to Three.js

The Three.js project includes extensions for the 3ds Max, Maya, and Blender 3D modeling programs to make exporting models to the Three.js JSON format easier. These extensions have some limitations; for example, some modifiers such as smoothing groups are not supported. There are two common alternatives to avoid these issues. The first is to export models to a format such as DAE and use the corresponding Three.js importer. Another approach is to export models to OBJ format and then run the Python converter script in the `utils/converters` folder to transform the model to Three.js JSON format. Choosing a file format is mostly a trade-off in file size (how long the file will take to retrieve) and initialization (how long the file will take to parse). You may need to test different formats for performance-sensitive projects.

The Python converters were written for Python 2.x and may not work in 3.x.

The most common problems that arise when importing models are due to not exporting all the required properties. In your modeling program's export dialog, if given a choice, make sure to check the boxes for these properties:

- Vertices
- Faces
- Normals
- Skinning / Materials / Texture Maps / Texture Coordinates / UVs / Colors
- Flip YZ
- Morph animation (if applicable)
- All meshes (if applicable)

Your modeling software may not have all these options, and you may need to check other boxes as well.

To be on the safe side, you may also want to make sure the model you're exporting is a top-level object rather than grouped with other things, that the model is not translated or rotated, that the scaling is set to 1, and that you've deleted the model's history.

Exporting from Three.js

Three.js provides several exporters in the `examples/js/exporters` folder that allow saving scenes or objects in various formats, including OBJ, STL, and JSON. Like with loaders, more or less any Three.js entity can be exported, but the most common approach is to export a complete mesh or scene. The `SceneExporter` tool is the most common tool here, and using it is fairly straightforward:

```
var exporter = new THREE.SceneExporter();
var output = JSON.stringify(exporter.parse(scene), null, "\t");
```

Then `output` value can be saved into a JSON file that `SceneLoader` can read later. The one major issue to watch out for is that custom properties won't get exported. That includes nonstandard properties added to object instances, properties provided by subclasses of Three.js classes, custom classes that don't inherit from Three.js classes, and anything that isn't part of the `scene`. If you need any of these things to be exported, you may be better off writing a custom exporter and importer, possibly starting with one of the ones Three.js provides.

Managing loaders

Right now, when our CTF map is initialized, we ask a loader to fetch the flag model. This works fine because the model is pretty small and we only have the one model to load. However, if we had many models or if they were bigger, we may notice them popping into the map when they finished loading, even after we've started playing. To fix this, larger projects should preload assets before the player can start playing the game. All that's required to do so is to disallow entering the map until the last model's callback has been executed. Unfortunately, if we have a lot of models and we have to load them one by one, it can be hard to keep track of how many models are remaining. Users may also lose interest if nothing is happening while models are loading.

Usually, this is resolved by loading all the models at once with the `SceneLoader`. The `SceneLoader` objects have a `callbackProgress` property that holds a function which is invoked after each object in the scene has completed loading. The callback takes two parameters, `progress` and `result`. The `progress` object has four numeric properties that can be used to display a progress bar: `totalModels`, `totalTextures`, `loadedModels`, and `loadedTextures`. The result object contains all of the entities that have been loaded so far, and it's also the value passed to the `onLoad` parameter of the loader's `load` callback when all loading has been completed.

Consider HTML like this for a loading bar, where the outer div has a defined width:

```
<div id="bar"><div id="progress"></div></div>
```

In this case, you might include code like this in a `callbackProgress` handler:

```
var total = progress.totalModels + progress.totalTextures,
    loaded = progress.loadedModels + progress.loadedTextures,
    progressBar = document.getElementById('progress');
progressBar.style.width = Math.round(100 * loaded / total) + '%';
```

If you can't use a `SceneLoader` or don't want to use it for other reasons, you will have to chain together your loaders manually. However, Three.js will start using **loading managers** in the future. Loading managers are just objects that work together with loaders to track when multiple resources have finished loading. The loading manager API is not yet stable as of Three.js version r61 and it is not implemented in many of the loaders.

Mesh animation

Using animated models is not very different from using normal models. There are essentially two types of animation to consider (in addition to manually changing the position of a mesh's geometry in Three.js).

> If all you need is to smoothly transition properties between different values—for example, changing the rotation of a door in order to animate it opening—you can use the Tween.js library at `https://github.com/sole/tween.js` to do so instead of animating the mesh itself. *Jerome Etienne* has a nice tutorial on doing this at `http://learningthreejs.com/blog/2011/08/17/tweenjs-for-smooth-animation/`.

Morph animation

Morph animation stores animation data as a sequence of positions. For example, if you had a cube with a *shrink* animation, your model could hold the positions of the vertices of the cube at full size and at the shrunk size. Then animation would consist of interpolating between those states during each rendering or **keyframe**. The data representing each state can hold either vertex targets or face normals.

To use morph animation, the easiest approach is to use a `THREE.MorphAnimMesh` class, which is a subclass of the normal mesh. In the following example, the highlighted lines should only be included if the model uses normals:

```
var loader = new THREE.JSONLoader();
loader.load('model.js', function(geometry) {
  var material = new THREE.MeshLambertMaterial({
    color: 0x000000,
    morphTargets: true,
    morphNormals: true,
  });
  if (geometry.morphColors && geometry.morphColors.length) {
    var colorMap = geometry.morphColors[0];
    for (var i = 0; i < colorMap.colors.length; i++) {
      geometry.faces[i].color = colorMap.colors[i];
    }
    material.vertexColors = THREE.FaceColors;
  }
  geometry.computeMorphNormals();
  var mesh = new THREE.MorphAnimMesh(geometry, material);
  mesh.duration = 5000; // in milliseconds
  scene.add(mesh);
  morphs.push(mesh);
});
```

The first thing we do is set our material to be aware that the mesh will be animated with the `morphTargets` properties and optionally with `morphNormal` properties. Next, we check whether colors will change during the animation, and set the mesh faces to their initial color if so (if you know your model doesn't have `morphColors`, you can leave out that block). Then the normals are computed (if we have them) and our `MorphAnimMesh` animation is created. We set the `duration` value of the full animation, and finally store the mesh in the global `morphs` array so that we can update it during our physics loop:

```
for (var i = 0; i < morphs.length; i++) {
  morphs[i].updateAnimation(delta);
}
```

Under the hood, the `updateAnimation` method just changes which set of positions in the animation the mesh should be interpolating between. By default, the animation will start immediately and loop indefinitely. To stop animating, just stop calling `updateAnimation`.

Skeletal animation

Skeletal animation moves a group of vertices in a mesh together by making them follow the movement of `bone`. This is generally easier to design because artists only have to move a few bones instead of potentially thousands of vertices. It's also typically less memory-intensive for the same reason.

To use morph animation, use a `THREE.SkinnedMesh` class, which is a subclass of the normal mesh:

```
var loader = new THREE.JSONLoader();
loader.load('model.js', function(geometry, materials) {
  for (var i = 0; i < materials.length; i++) {
    materials[i].skinning = true;
  }
  var material = new THREE.MeshFaceMaterial(materials);
  THREE.AnimationHandler.add(geometry.animation);
  var mesh = new THREE.SkinnedMesh(geometry, material, false);
  scene.add(mesh);
  var animation = new THREE.Animation(mesh, geometry.animation.name);
  animation.interpolationType = THREE.AnimationHandler.LINEAR; // or
  CATMULLROM for cubic splines (ease-in-out)
  animation.play();
});
```

The model we're using in this example already has materials, so unlike in the morph animation examples, we have to change the existing materials instead of creating a new one. For skeletal animation we have to enable **skinning**, which refers to how the materials are wrapped around the mesh as it moves. We use the `THREE.AnimationHandler` utility to track where we are in the current animation and a `THREE.SkinnedMesh` utility to properly handle our model's bones. Then we use the mesh to create a new `THREE.Animation` and play it. The animation's `interpolationType` determines how the mesh transitions between states. If you want cubic spline easing (slow then fast then slow), use `THREE.AnimationHandler.CATMULLROM` instead of the `LINEAR` easing.

We also need to update the animation in our physics loop:

```
THREE.AnimationHandler.update(delta);
```

It is possible to use both skeletal and morph animations at the same time. In this case, the best approach is to treat the animation as skeletal and manually update the mesh's `morphTargetInfluences` array as demonstrated in `examples/webgl_animation_skinning_morph.html` in the Three.js project.

Particle systems

Now that our flags are in place and we've learned how to manage the resources we'll need to decorate our world, let's add some additional visual effects. The first type of effect we'll look at is particle systems.

Particles are planes that always face the camera, usually grouped together into a *system* to create some effect like fire or steam. They are essential for creating great visuals like this colorful heart:

Particles from examples/webgl_particles_shapes.html with shapes by zz85

Capturing the flag

We'd like to set off a celebratory fireworks-style display when the player captures a flag, so if you haven't already done so, go ahead and add the mechanics of capturing flags. The core logic should be in a function we'll call for each player in our physics loop:

```
function checkHasFlag(unit) {
  var otherFlag = unit.team === TEAMS.R ? TEAMS.B.flag : TEAMS.R.flag;
  if (unit.hasFlag) {
    var flag = unit.team === TEAMS.R ? TEAMS.R.flag : TEAMS.B.flag;
    if (flag.mesh.visible && isPlayerInCell(flag.row, flag.col)) {
      otherFlag.mesh.traverse(function(node) {
        node.visible = true;
      });
      unit.hasFlag = false;
    }
  }
  else if (otherFlag.mesh.visible && isPlayerInCell(otherFlag.row,
  otherFlag.col)) {
    otherFlag.mesh.traverse(function(node) {
      node.visible = false;
    });
    unit.hasFlag = true;
  }
}
```

If the player has the opponent's flag, we're checking if they're standing on their own flag so that they can score; if the player doesn't have the flag, we're checking if they're standing on the other flag so that they can steal it. When a flag is stolen it is marked as invisible, and it is marked as visible again when it is returned. (The code for this is not included in the preceding example, but flags also need to be returned when a flag carrier dies.)

Objects' `visible` property is a Boolean controlling whether or not they are rendered. In the WebGL renderer, setting this property does not affect child objects, though it does affect child objects in other renderers. This is important to know for multipart meshes, which are often imported in a hierarchy. To set the visibility for an object and all its children, you can use the `traverse` method, which invokes a callback for each object in the hierarchy:

```
object.traverse(function(node) {
  node.visible = false;
});
```

Particles and Sprites

`CanvasRenderer` and `WebGLRenderer` use different objects to represent individual particles. When using canvas, use `THREE.Particle`:

```
var material = new THREE.ParticleBasicMaterial({
  color: 0x660000,
  map: null, // or an image texture
});
var particle = new THREE.Particle(material);
```

As you can see, particles are basically just made up of a color or an image. Similarly, when using WebGL, use `THREE.Sprite`:

```
var material = new THREE.SpriteMaterial({
  color: 0x660000,
  map: null, // or an image texture
  opacity: 1.0,
  blending: THREE.AdditiveBlending,
});
var sprite = new THREE.Sprite(material);
```

Sprites are basically the same as particles except that they also support different blending modes. Supported blending modes are shown in the following screenshot:

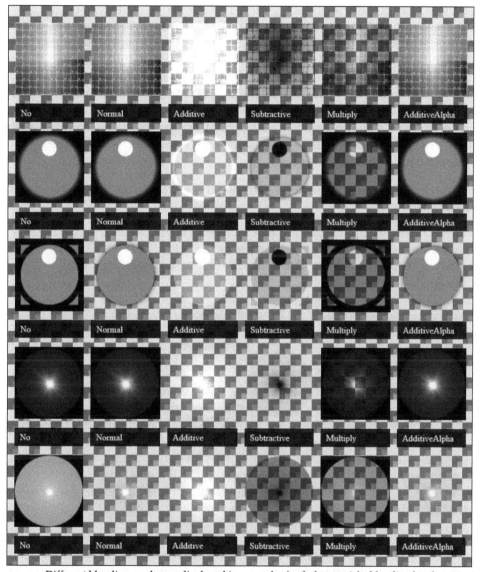

Different blending modes, as displayed in examples/webgl_materials_blending.html

In both cases, you can use the position and scale vectors the same way we've been using them for meshes, except that scale.z has no effect.

Particle systems

Particle systems are a way to create and manage lots of particles at once. They use geometry to place a particle on each vertex. This has the benefit that you can use built-in tools we've already seen to manipulate the geometry. For example, you can use a particle system with imported animated geometry. However, they also have several limitations. First, creating dynamic effects can be difficult because you have to code them manually, for example by updating the velocity of each individual particle in each frame. Second, you can't add and remove particles (although you can set their opacity to zero), so you have to pre-allocate as many particles as you might need. Third, you can only use a single material per particle system, so all the particles in a given system will have the same image, size, and rotation (though you can independently change their color).

For the purposes of our CTF game, we'll create a celebratory particle system when we create our flags:

```
var geometry = new THREE.IcosahedronGeometry(200, 2);
var mat = new THREE.ParticleBasicMaterial({
  color: type === 'R' ? TEAMS.R.color : TEAMS.B.color,
  size: 10,
});
var system = new THREE.ParticleSystem(geometry, mat);
system.sortParticles = true;
system.position.set(x, VERTICAL_UNIT * 0.5, z);
scene.add(system);
```

This will create small particles in a roughly spherical shape around the flag we're initializing. The `sortParticles` property indicates whether particles should be sorted by depth so that particles closer to the camera appear in front of those that are farther away. Sometimes sorting particles can create a strange popping effect when particles are moving and overlapping, so you may want to test and see what looks better to you. Additionally, enabling sorting when you have many thousands of particles can be computationally expensive, though it should be fine with the few hundred particles in our example.

To complete the effect, we actually want to make the system invisible with `system.visible = false`, then temporarily make it visible when a flag is captured later. Also, our particles will also be more interesting if they move around. We can rotate the whole particle system by changing its rotation vector:

```
system.rotation.y += delta * 1.5;
```

You can see the result in the following screenshot:

A celebratory particle effect

We can also move the geometry's vertices directly if we want. To do this, we first need to set `geometry.dynamic = true` before creating the particle system, then set `geometry.verticesNeedUpdate = true` every time we change vertex positions.

We don't need to do this for our game, but it's also possible to change the color of individual particles by changing the `geometry.colors` array. You can fill this array with one color for each vertex (at the same index) and that color will be blended with the color or image of the particle's material.

Some things you may want to do with particles can get quite complicated. For example, to simulate spray from a waterfall, you might use particles with some physics applied. To simplify similar advanced use cases, two libraries have emerged. One of them, called **Sparks**, is actually included with Three.js in the examples/js folder. It's also available online at https://github.com/zz85/sparks.js and is written by *zz85*. A newer library written by *Luke Moody* and *Lee Stemkoski* is available at https://github.com/squarefeet/ShaderParticleEngine, and while relatively untested, the API is simpler and it's somewhat lighter in weight.

Sound

Although Three.js is a graphics library, there is an experimental THREE.AudioObject class at examples/js/AudioObject.js that uses the Web Audio API to support 3D sound effects. This object inherits from Object3D so it can be attached to other objects and placed in the world. It is designed to use spatially accurate 3D sound. The main caveat is that the class only works with Chrome as of Three.js version r61 due to browser incompatibilities.

 Like with external models, audio is loaded with AJAX, so local file URLs won't work by default.

That said, let's go ahead and try adding some cheering sounds when a flag is captured. First, we'll create our AudioObject instances when we initialize our flags:

```
var cheering = new THREE.AudioObject('cheering.ogg', 0, 1, false);
scene.add(cheering);
```

This code creates an object to play the cheering.ogg file with a volume of 0, a playback rate of 1, and no looping. We set the volume to zero initially because AudioObject plays the sound immediately, and we only want it to play when we capture a flag. To that end, let's trigger the sound to play when we capture a flag:

```
THREE.AudioObject.call(cheering, 'cheering.ogg', 1, 1, false);
```

AudioObject does not provide a way to play a sound again, so we have to call the constructor to force it to do that. This time, we set the volume to 1. The crowd goes wild!

If you set the final parameter to true instead of false, you can also use this to play looping sounds or even music.

Renderer effects and postprocessing

Sometimes, effects that change the entire display can give a game or area a lot of personality. Three.js supports two major kinds of effects: renderer and postprocessing.

Renderer effects can be found in `examples/js/effects`. They change what the renderer outputs, usually by rendering the scene multiple times with different settings. For example, the Anaglyph effect produces the familiar red-and-blue shadows that work with 3D glasses to make the scene pop out of the screen, and it does this by rendering the scene once for the left eye, once for the right eye, and once combined. Setting this up is easy:

```
effect = new THREE.AnaglyphEffect(renderer);
effect.setSize(renderer.domElement.width, renderer.domElement.height);
```

Then just call `effect.render(scene, camera)` instead of `renderer.render(scene, camera)`. All of the other renderer effects work the same way except the ASCII effect, which requires adding a separate canvas so it can render the scene to text characters.

Postprocessing effects work by applying a GLSL shader over the scene. There are many shaders that can be used in the `examples/js`, `examples/js/postprocessing`, and `examples/js/shaders` folders. Most of these are just fun, but a few are useful in games. The **DOF** (**depth-of-field**) effect, for example, blurs distant objects and brings closer ones into focus.

The `EffectComposer` in `examples/js/postprocessing` makes applying post-processing easier and allows using multiple effects. For example, to use the `EdgeShader`, start by adding the necessary files in your HTML:

```
<script src="EdgeShader.js"></script>
<script src="CopyShader.js"></script>
<script src="ShaderPass.js"></script>
<script src="RenderPass.js"></script>
<script src="MaskPass.js"></script>
<script src="EffectComposer.js"></script>
```

Then set up the effect:

```
composer = new THREE.EffectComposer(renderer);
composer.addPass(new THREE.RenderPass(scene, camera));
var effect = new THREE.ShaderPass(THREE.EdgeShader);
effect.uniforms['aspect'].value.x = renderer.domElement.width;
effect.uniforms['aspect'].value.y = renderer.domElement.height;
composer.addPass(effect);
effect = new THREE.ShaderPass(THREE.CopyShader);
effect.renderToScreen = true;
composer.addPass(effect);
```

This code requests two postprocessing rendering passes during which the edge and copy shaders will both be applied. The edge effect requires knowledge of the canvas size, and the effects will be rendered after the copy shader is applied. The final step is to replace our `renderer.render(scene, camera)` call with `composer.render()`, and we get a pretty dramatic result, as you can see in the next screenshot:

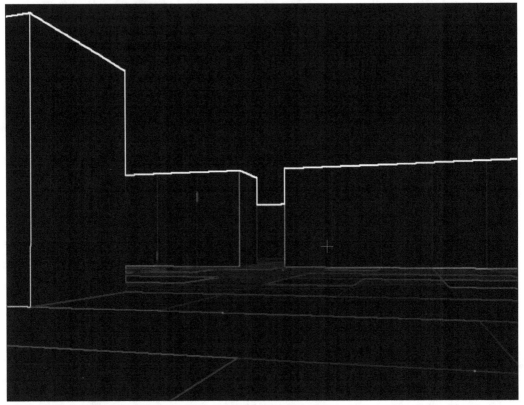

Our game with the edge shader postprocessor

As previously mentioned, shaders are written in GLSL instead of JavaScript, and they can get pretty complex. As a result, we won't talk about how to write them here. However, you can browse and fork some shaders other people have written at `https://glsl.heroku.com/`. Three.js author *Mr.doob* has also written a shader editor at `http://www.mrdoob.com/projects/glsl_sandbox/`, and *Thibaut Despoulain* has written one as well at `http://shdr.bkcore.com/`. Note that shaders can be used to display pretty much anything, and most shaders don't make sense as postprocessors.

Summary

In this chapter, we learned how to manage 3D models and animation. We also explored particle systems, sound, and visual effects. Additionally, we used what we learned to transform our first-person shooter game from *Chapter 3, Exploring and Interacting* into a Capture-the-Flag game. In the next chapter, we'll discuss game design concepts, workflow processes, performance considerations, and networking.

5
Design and Development

While other chapters have focused on the Three.js API and how to use it to build games, this chapter discusses how to make *good* games using Three.js and the Web as a platform. We'll use what we've learned so far as a foundation to explore game design concepts and development processes, investigate performance considerations, and introduce JavaScript-based game networking.

Game design for the Web

Building games based on WebGL that match or exceed console quality should be possible, and doing so is a worthy goal. Additionally, building games for the Web presents an opportunity to take advantage of features that aren't possible for desktop and console games, although there are also a few drawbacks.

For example, you can build mechanics around having game data in URLs. Beyond just indicating save/load points, URLs could encode pickups, locations, random seeds, or other information. Add sharing to the mix and suddenly you have the ability for users to e-mail or tweet a link to their friends and have them drop instantly into the same point in your game. Unlike console games, web games can build on viral dynamics, the ubiquity of browsers, and low barriers to entry to attract more users and introduce new gameplay. You might imagine collaborative puzzle games that require a certain number of players to be completed — a concept that wouldn't be reliable for an expensive console game.

At the same time, gamers who buy an expensive console game are probably more likely to put in some effort to get over an initial learning curve. Unless users pay for your game up front, it's important to be conscious of the fact that users can leave your game just as easily as they arrived. Gaming has always been about balancing difficulty with engagement; it's the same formula, but it's more important than ever to consider the amount of time between hitting your landing page and that first taste of sweet satisfaction.

Web-based games also benefit from a strong tradition of APIs and integrations. Of course console games can also use APIs, but by definition, web-based games can typically rely on players having an Internet connection, so you can imagine gameplay elements such as imagery from Google Earth, location names and tips based on Foursquare data, and AI characters who actively use social networks. In particular, you can easily integrate payment processing into your games, perhaps even superimposed over a cash register or ATM, and reasonably expect that many users will have access to a keyboard that will let them type in their credit card information more easily than they could with a joystick. This opens the door to non-traditional payment methods that don't require charging up-front for games, more akin to the way mobile games often make money from in-app sales.

Additionally, webcam and microphone access is growing rapidly among laptop users, and Chrome and Firefox now support these peripherals with the WebRTC API. Potential uses of this technology go beyond simple chatting. Ambient sound could be detected and used to adjust the tempo of game music. With some machine vision or perhaps a Leap Motion device, users could interact directly with the game by waving their hands instead of manipulating a mouse. Imagine a game of Roller Coaster Tycoon where you could literally pick up visitors and fling them to the other side of your park! There are lots of other cool uses for machine vision as well. *John Carmack* (lead programmer of Doom and Quake among other iconic games) recently suggested running garbage collection when the user blinks. Research at MIT has shown that webcam video can be used to accurately identify visitors' heart rates, which could allow games to adjust their pace to match (or compensate for) users' excitement (http://people.csail.mit.edu/mrub/vidmag/). And hand-tracking technology is already being used for 3D modeling, game development, and even rocket design.

Other external devices such as the Oculus Rift augmented reality headset can be supported for deeper integration into your environment. (Three.js actually includes a controller for the Oculus Rift in the examples/js/controls folder). For example, mobile phones can be used as controllers for web games as described at http://cykod.com/blog/post/2011-08-using-nodejs-and-your-phone-to-control-a-browser-game and http://blog.artlogic.com/2013/06/21/phone-to-browser-html5-gaming-using-node-js-and-socket-io/. Experimental support for traditional USB game controllers exists in some browsers as well; one library to help with that is available at http://www.gamepadjs.com/. Phones and tablets could even be used as an additional screen—perhaps for a minimap, inventory list, or rearview mirror.

That said, because the Web is universally available, consider what devices may be accessing your game and what constraints they may have. Varied screen sizes and resolutions are nothing new, but touch controls in particular can present challenges for 3D games. Still, applying traditional web development techniques to games can yield creative solutions. For instance, taking the approach of graceful degradation / progressive enhancement, mobile users could be delivered a spectator view or some other reduced version of the game. Alternatively, you could provide onscreen controls when keyboards and mice aren't available, perhaps with the HTML5 Virtual Game Controller library (`https://github.com/austinhallock/html5-virtual-game-controller`).

One final point to think about: Three.js-driven games can integrate smoothly with existing websites. For example, most games need menus, and it's much easier to create them in HTML than in 3D. Don't feel like your entire application needs to display exclusively on the canvas. On the other hand, if you want to get creative, you can actually embed HTML inside your Three.js environment. You can read more about how to do this at `http://learningthreejs.com/blog/2013/04/30/closing-the-gap-between-html-and-webgl/` and `http://jensarps.de/2013/07/02/html-elements-in-webgl-recursion/`.

Performance

In some ways, performance considerations for 3D games in browsers are pretty similar to those for consoles and desktop games. The biggest difference is that all resources must (at least initially) be streamed to the client instead of read from a disk. For complex 3D games with gigabytes of assets, overcoming this limitation for low-bandwidth clients can be a serious challenge.

As legendary programmer *Donald Knuth* wrote:

"Premature optimization is the root of all evil."

This section discusses best practices and suggestions to get great performance out of your game, but before expending significant effort, you should measure and test your application to see where the bottlenecks are and whether the effort is worthwhile.

Bandwidth/network constraints

To combat bandwidth constraints, the first thing you should do is apply traditional optimizations which web developers have been using for years: compress the content your server sends with `gzip`, combine and minify JavaScript to minimize the number of requests the browser has to make to the server, optimize your images, enable the Keep-Alive header, serve assets from a limited number of domains, and use headers to leverage browser caching, among other techniques.

Optimizing websites in general is a particularly detailed topic, but this section mostly sticks to explaining optimizations specifically for games. If you are interested in learning more about **Web Performance Optimization (WPO)**, start with these rules from Google and Yahoo!:

- `https://developers.google.com/speed/docs/best-practices/rules_intro`
- `http://developer.yahoo.com/performance/rules.html`

However, complex games won't be able to rely on browser caching for user return visits because browsers have limits on the maximum amount of memory cached resources can consume across all websites. Your game's resources will be pushed out of the cache as the user navigates other websites, and the cache size may be too small for all your resources anyway. As a result, the next place to look for optimizations is caching inside of your game in order to minimize the number of server requests that need to be made. This can be done in three ways. First, you can store resources in other caches. The IndexedDB API (`https://developer.mozilla.org/en-US/docs/IndexedDB`) supports storing files, and the Web Storage API (`https://developer.mozilla.org/en-US/docs/Web/Guide/API/DOM/Storage#localStorage`) supports storing strings (including JSON, so you can store exported Three.js objects). Chrome also supports the FileSystem API (`http://www.html5rocks.com/en/tutorials/file/filesystem/`) which can manage a sandboxed local filesystem. Second, you can reduce the total number of resources you need by generating some of them on the client. For example, if you need similar textures in different colors, it might make sense to modify those textures dynamically on the client rather than ask the server for multiple images. Or, if you can describe the way a mesh should animate with a system of equations, you might consider manually animating it on the client instead of sending animation data. Third, you can make sure your code is structured in a way that allows reusing resources instead of requesting them repeatedly. For example, if two meshes use the same texture, you should try to load the texture once instead of twice.

Finally, you can use a binary format for imported meshes that has a higher compression ratio than standard text-based files in order to reduce the size of assets the server needs to send to the client. To do so, you should export your meshes to Wavefront OBJ / MTL files, and then use the converter script at `utils/converters/obj/convert_obj_three.py` to generate a file that the `THREE.BinaryLoader` can import. (Instructions for running the script are at the top of the file.)

In addition to reducing the total size of resources that need to be retrieved from a server, you can try to load as much data as possible while the user doesn't need to see it. For example, if players enter your game from a menu, you may be able to start loading while the player is navigating the menu rather than waiting until they click to start the game. You can also wait to load parts of your scene that won't be visible initially until after the player has entered the game, in order to let the player start playing as quickly as possible. For example, linear mission-based games can wait to load parts of the map until the player reaches certain checkpoints. Just make sure you have a fallback plan if resources are loading slowly and the player reaches your unloaded area too early. You might want to have a door that won't open until the resources are loaded. You could also just pause the game momentarily when the player is in a transitional location.

Level of detail

Similarly, you can load low-poly meshes and low-resolution textures when the user starts playing the game and replace them with higher-detail assets during gameplay, either when the larger assets are loaded or when the user gets close enough to them to see the improved detail. The latter technique is called **Level-of-Detail (LOD)**, and Three.js has built-in support for it using the `THREE.LOD` object. For example, we could modify the spinning shape example we built in *Chapter 1, Hello, Three.js*, to change the detail of our sphere depending on how close to it we are. First we need to change how we add the mesh to the scene:

```
geometry = [
  [new THREE.IcosahedronGeometry(200, 4), 50],
  [new THREE.IcosahedronGeometry(200, 3), 300],
  [new THREE.IcosahedronGeometry(200, 2), 1000],
  [new THREE.IcosahedronGeometry(200, 1), 2000],
  [new THREE.IcosahedronGeometry(200, 0), 8000],
];
material = new THREE.MeshNormalMaterial();

lod = new THREE.LOD();
```

```
for (var i = 0; i < geometry.length; i++) {
  var mesh = new THREE.Mesh(geometry[i][0], material);
  lod.addLevel(mesh, geometry[i][1]);
}
scene.add(lod);
```

The LOD object stores objects of different complexities along with the distances at which higher-detail versions should be used. To make the mesh change detail when the camera moves closer or farther away, we'll update the LOD object in the animation loop:

```
scene.traverse(function(object) {
  if (object instanceof THREE.LOD) {
    object.position.z = 2500 * Math.cos(Date.now() / 1000);
    object.update(camera);
  }
});
```

We added a little bit of movement here so that we can see the detail change. Let's move the camera so that we can see the movement better by setting camera. position.z = 3000. Now you should be able to see the detail change dynamically, as shown in the following screenshot:

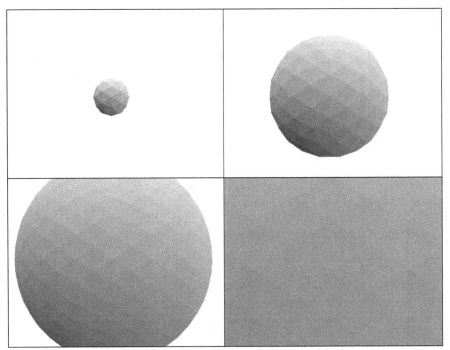

A sphere with increasing detail as the camera gets closer

Rendering optimizations

Three.js has built-in support for other detail-related optimizations as well in order to make processing faster. **Culling**, the process of excluding hidden objects from rendering, is a common example. Three.js does **view frustum culling** based on bounding spheres, meaning it will avoid spending valuable compute time calculating visual information about objects that are off screen. It also does **backface culling** by default, which hides the back side of mesh faces. However, it doesn't do **occlusion culling**, meaning it doesn't know not to render an object that is in front of the camera but obscured by another object that is closer to the camera. The implication of these optimizations is that large meshes should often be split into several smaller ones to reduce computation if only part of the large mesh is on the screen, and you don't get any benefits by default from having short viewable distances. This simple change might be sufficient for top-down games where few objects are obscured by other objects. Other games, such as first-person shooters where buildings or terrain can block long view distances, may need to compensate in other ways. For example, if you have really large or detailed worlds, you may want to work on manual occlusion culling. Game engines typically do this using a technique called **depth testing**, but a simpler approach that can work for enclosed layouts (such as the insides of buildings) is to create invisible cubes encompassing different zones in the world based on view distances and then toggle the visibility of meshes inside those zones when the player gets close enough.

We've already discussed the advantages of merging geometry in *Chapter 2, Building a World*, but you can get additional performance benefit out of transforming static geometry into `BufferGeometry`. `BufferGeometry` typically renders faster than standard `Geometry` because it uses a data structure that is closer to what will get passed to the GPU instead of one that is easy for humans to understand. As a result, it is harder to manipulate, but it works well if you know your geometry won't change. The easiest way to use `BufferGeometry` is to convert from existing `Geometry` using the utility in `examples/js/BufferGeometryUtils.js`:

```
THREE.BufferGeometryUtils.fromGeometry(geometry);
```

You can use the result with meshes the same way you would use normal geometry.

Another powerful optimization is changing the resolution of the canvas. Assuming `renderer` and `camera` are globals, you can use this function to do so:

```
var resize = (function() {
  var canvas = renderer.domElement;
  canvas.style.width = canvas.width + 'px';
  canvas.style.height = canvas.height + 'px';
  var originalWidth = canvas.width;
  var originalHeight = canvas.height;
```

```
    return function(scale) {
      canvas.width = Math.round(originalWidth*scale);
      canvas.height = Math.round(originalHeight*scale);
      camera.aspect = canvas.width / canvas.height;
      camera.updateProjectionMatrix();
      renderer.setSize(canvas.width, canvas.height);
    }
  })();
```

You can use this function by calling `resize(0.5)`, for example, which will allow the renderer to paint only `0.5*0.5 = 25%` of the pixels it would paint at full resolution, even though the canvas will take up the same amount of space on the screen. (The `scale` parameter is always relative to the canvas' original size.) This works because canvases are basically just images. In the same way that you can style an image to be larger in CSS without changing its actual size, you can style a canvas to be larger too. In our `resize` function, we first reduce the actual size of the canvas by changing its `width` and `height` attributes, then scale it back up using the CSS width and height styles. The result is that the canvas takes up the same amount of screen space that it did originally, but each actual pixel is displayed larger. This significantly reduces the amount of computation required to render a scene, although the scene will be blurrier.

Changing the resolution of the canvas affects how you need to compute where the user clicks. You should track the canvas' current scale and adjust the screen-space vector in our click method from *Chapter 3, Exploring and Interacting*, accordingly:

```
var vector = new THREE.Vector3(
  scale *  renderer.devicePixelRatio * (event.pageX -
  this.offsetLeft) / this.width * 2 - 1,
  scale * -renderer.devicePixelRatio * (event.pageY -
  this.offsetTop) / this.height * 2 + 1,
  0.5
    );
```

Techniques that compromise visual detail in favor of speed are especially useful when combined with frame-rate testing. If the frame rate dips below a certain threshold for more than a given percent of the time in a certain testing period, you may want to reduce your game's detail. (You should figure out what your bottleneck is before implementing this approach. If your frame rates are low because your physics loop takes a long time to run, reducing visual detail may not help much.)

If physics is your bottleneck, you can run your physics at a lower frame rate than your rendering as discussed in *Chapter 3, Exploring and Interacting*. You may also want to consider using the Web Worker API (`https://developer.mozilla.org/en-US/docs/Web/Guide/Performance/Using_web_workers`) to execute JavaScript code in parallel. This can allow calculating movement and collision without blocking the rendering. The Physi.js library introduced in *Chapter 3, Exploring and Interacting*, does this automatically.

Battery life and GPU memory

Although bandwidth/network speed and processing time are the factors that usually affect the performance of Three.js games the most, battery life and memory constraints may also come into play. For hardcore games, you may be able to assume the user is plugged in, but more casual games should be aware that more processing typically equates to more battery drain. On the memory front, the question is less about storage space and more about the graphics card having a limited amount of embedded memory with which it can perform fast computations. The main thing you can do to limit how much of the GPU's onboard memory you consume is to use compressed textures. (Normally, images such as JPGs and PNGs are decompressed before being sent to the GPU, but compressed textures use a special format that allows the GPU to hold them in embedded memory in a compressed state. Since the compression only matters for the GPU, it doesn't actually save network bandwidth.) Three.js supports compressed textures in DDS format. You can import DDS textures into Three.js like this:

```
var texture = THREE.ImageUtils.loadCompressedTexture(imagePath);
```

The resulting `texture` value can be treated the same way normal images are treated; you can use it as the value for the `map` property of materials, for example, and Three.js will automatically know how to handle it.

 To create DDS images, you can use a plugin for Gimp (`https://code.google.com/p/gimp-dds/`) or Photoshop (`https://developer.nvidia.com/nvidia-texture-tools-adobe-photoshop`).

Performance-measuring tools

Finally, there are a number of useful tools for measuring JavaScript performance. Conveniently, the original author of Three.js has written a library called Stats.js (`https://github.com/mrdoob/stats.js`) for tracking frame rates, the most crucial performance statistic for games. For comprehensive tracing, Google's Web Tracing Framework (`http://google.github.io/tracing-framework/index.html`) is hard to beat, and it even has an example for tracing a WebGL game. You can also easily get some statistics about onscreen geometry with the RenderStats library from *Jerome Etienne* (`https://github.com/jeromeetienne/threex.rendererstats`).

For brute-force debugging, you may also want to try the console-extras library, which makes it easier to log information about things that happen in the main game loop without dumping thousands of messages (`https://github.com/unconed/console-extras.js`).

Networking and multiplayer

Game networking is hard because the goal of networking is to keep game state in sync across multiple devices, but network latency prevents devices from communicating fast enough to keep that state from being occasionally inconsistent. Additionally, floating point rounding errors create indeterminate results across devices for the same set of input (this is where the timing and movement techniques discussed in *Chapter 3, Exploring and Interacting* come into play, since small differences in precision can result in huge differences over time). As a result, networking code becomes a process of reconciling differences.

There are basically two different approaches to networking depending on the requirements of the game. RTS and turn-based games usually use an approach called **lock-step**, which is a peer-to-peer model in which each computer in a match sends its commands to all the other computers in the match. The main strength of this model is that only a small amount of data (the players' commands) needs to be sent over the network, so it is useful when the game state is huge (for example, when there are thousands of units in a map). However, running a game in lock-step depends on all players having an identical copy of the game state, which is a great idea in theory but is difficult to maintain for several reasons. First, although the JavaScript specification states that floating point calculations should be deterministic, in practice there may be subtle differences across implementations that could prevent clients from being in sync.

Second, all clients will see the game run at the speed of the most-latent client because commands from each player must be collected before advancing in order to ensure synchronicity. As a result, extra precautions must be taken to keep clients from cheating by pretending to have higher latency and waiting for the other computers' commands before making a decision. The latency issue also creates trouble when one machine is taking a particularly long time to return a command. In such a situation, the game may have to drop that player. Since the reason for using lock-step is that the entire game state is too large to transfer over the network while maintaining synchronicity, it may not be feasible for a player to join (or re-join) after a game has already started.

The other approach to game networking is a client-server prediction model, which usually works like this:

1. The client triggers some input (such as pressing a key or moving the mouse) that changes the game state.
2. The client input is sent to the server.
3. Optionally, the server forwards the input to the other clients.
4. The server processes the inputs it receives from all players, reconciles them, and produces a new, authoritative description of the game's state at a specific time.
5. If the server forwarded other clients' inputs, the clients receive those inputs and continue updating the local game state by predicting what the server thinks the state should be.
6. The server periodically sends the latest complete description of the authoritative game state to each client.
7. The client adjusts its state to sync with the server's official state.

The main difference here compared to lock-step is that clients can advance the game independently, and the entire game state can be sent from the server to ensure each player sees something pretty close to what the others see. This is a better model for action games like FPSs or games with many players like MMOs because players generally experience less dramatic latency effects.

To reduce the lag that gamers can feel, we design the client-server communication to be asynchronous because waiting for the new game state from the server can take a long time due to network latency. Since we try to keep running the game locally while we wait for the server, we need to adjust the client when we do finally get an authoritative update from the server. Adjusting the client can be tricky, though. First of all, by the time we get a response from the server, the state it sends us will be in the past. To deal with this, we'll need to keep track of all player input since the last time we got an official server update, rewind the game to the newly received authoritative game state, and then replay any more recent input on top of that. The result will be our latest guess of what the server thinks the game state should be at the current time, which will likely be slightly different than what we've actually been showing the player. We could just snap the current game state to our ideal game state, but that would make the game seem jittery since things might spontaneously teleport. Instead, if the differences between states are small enough, clients should interpolate between their current state and their projected ideal state. If we drift too far away, we can snap back to the server state, but otherwise we'll lag a few frames in order to ensure smoothness. Snapping happens most often with complex physics interactions or when players collide.

Ideally, we'd like to just send players' inputs to the clients because they're smaller than the full game state (so they take up fewer network packets). This might be the only sane way to handle MMO games with potentially thousands of players. However, this can cause drifting over time due to floating point rounding error, so it may not be accurate enough to be the only solution for intense action games like first-person shooters. As a compromise, inputs can be sent frequently and the full game state sent only periodically; then clients can use the inputs to predict how the game should progress.

Of course, not all physics is driven by user input. If your game has gameplay-affecting nature-driven physics such as wind or avalanches, you may need to have the server simulate the physics without client prediction, and clients will just have to deal with some latency. On the other hand, you can simulate some physics entirely on the client. For example, it doesn't really matter if the clouds in the sky are in exactly the same position on each client since they're typically just decorative.

The game state tracked by the server usually includes, at a minimum, the position and velocity of all movable actors, a unique identifier for the version of the state, and a timestamp. The server does not need to send a full scene export to every client since that would be too expensive. However, the server does need to simulate the full scene in order to accurately update the game state.

For more information on lock-step, check out `http://www.altdevblogaday.com/2011/07/09/synchronous-rts-engines-and-a-tale-of-desyncs/` and `http://www.altdevblogaday.com/2011/07/24/synchronous-rts-engines-2-sync-harder/`.

For more information about client-server prediction, check out `http://gafferongames.com/networking-for-game-programmers/what-every-programmer-needs-to-know-about-game-networking/`.

To learn about interpolating between authoritative and client states, see `http://www.gamedev.net/page/resources/_/technical/multiplayer-and-network-programming/defeating-lag-with-cubic-splines-r914`.

There is a great Google Tech Talk by *Rob Hawkes* on HTML5 multiplayer game development with many tips about overcoming common pitfalls. You can watch it at `https://www.youtube.com/watch?v=zj1qTrpuXJ8`.

Technologies

The Web Sockets API (`https://developer.mozilla.org/en-US/docs/WebSockets`) is the most practical way to maintain a fast connection with a game server in JavaScript, and the easiest way to use web sockets is to use node.js (`http://nodejs.org/`) on the server with the socket.io library (`http://socket.io/`). Node.js allows JavaScript to be a first-class server-side language, so you can write your game code once and worry less about differences between the server-side and client-side simulations. It's also mentally easier to write both the server-side and client-side code in a single language.

Web sockets are the best we can do at the moment because JavaScript doesn't have as much control over how it accesses the Internet as desktop and console games do, for security reasons. Web sockets are actually reasonably good, but they are based on **TCP**, which is a common way to access the Internet that ensures reliability but occasionally causes delays. Many desktop and console games that use client-server prediction use **UDP** to access the Internet instead, which serves the same purpose as TCP but compromises data-integrity guarantees in favor of minimal delays.

Voxel.js (`http://voxeljs.com/`) is a good example of a networked game framework using Three.js. If you are building a Minecraft-style game, it is a great place to start. For more information and code examples on writing game networking code in JavaScript with Socket.io and Node.js, there is a good article at `http://buildnewgames.com/real-time-multiplayer/`. It uses a 2D game as an example, but everything applies cleanly to 3D games as well.

Anticheating

Stopping cheaters in multiplayer games is a hard problem in general, and it's particularly difficult in JavaScript for three reasons. One, it's very difficult to detect whether client input is automated or their display has changed illegally; two, JavaScript code is relatively hard to obfuscate and validate without significant performance penalties; and three, cheating programs can directly and easily override your client code. As a result, anticheating efforts typically focus on moving as much logic as possible from the client to the server, detecting unusual patterns of client activity, minimizing the benefits of cheating, and perhaps creating just enough annoying barriers to cheating that some aspiring cheaters give up. Common methods include:

- Only letting the client send whitelisted inputs to the server, not arbitrary values; this allows a trusted computer (the server) to do important calculations and avoids letting cheaters make illegal requests such as `addPoints(1000000)`

- Tracking how long the user plays the game; if a user plays for 48 hours straight, they're worth investigating

- Tracking the amount of time that passes between user actions; if a user clicks on the same part of the screen every 10 minutes (suspiciously accurate) or 16 milliseconds (suspiciously fast), they might be automating their behavior

- Reporting snapping, the behavior in first-person shooters of instantly turning to shoot at a target as soon as there is nothing in the way, even when that target wasn't onscreen, and never missing

- Making debugging harder, for example by disabling console logging (`console = {}`) and wrapping your entire client-side code in a closure to prevent any global variables from being easily available to cheaters' scripts

- Making it easy for users to report abuse

This is certainly not an exhaustive list, and it's very difficult to stop cheaters entirely, but these suggestions are a reasonable place to start.

It's generally considered poor form to prevent client-side cheating in single-player modes, except when it comes to artifacts that other players can see, such as high scores.

Development processes

Whether you're an individual who builds games as a hobby or a developer for a large game publisher, you can benefit from following a number of best practices adopted from JavaScript development for the Web and game development on other platforms. You can also build Three.js-based games without deviating too far from your favorite game development processes.

JavaScript best practices

In previous chapters, we haven't been very concerned with the high-level structure of our code. We wrote some examples as single HTML files, and we split the FPS and CTF projects into separate files, but for polished games we should be more careful, especially when working with teams. General coding lessons apply:

- Keep assets in folders by file type/purpose. For example, at a high level you might have folders such as css, js, images, models, and sounds. Within the js folder, organize JavaScript files by purpose; keep library, source, and production code separate.

- Avoid putting code that directly handles user input event listeners in class constructors, because that makes them harder to reuse and extend.

- Use separate files for configuration/constants that you can fiddle with to adjust how the game *feels*.

- Detect features instead of browsers, since different browser versions support different features and some features can be toggled on or off in browser settings.

- Avoid using setTimeout and setInterval for timers in the animation loop because having a lot of separate timers can cause performance issues. Instead, check how much time has passed in your animation loop, for example, using Date.now() or THREE.Clock.

 If your game can pause, make sure you're not including time elapsed while paused.

- Though it may feel natural to write the entire application in JavaScript, try to avoid creating new DOM in JavaScript. Doing so is slow, and there's a reason HTML and CSS exist. (Also, don't be afraid to use HTML and CSS; sometimes that's a much easier solution than, say, writing a custom shader.)

- Use a style guide. Which one you choose is not especially important, but maintaining a consistent style helps avoid silly mistakes that are otherwise vulnerable to JavaScript's dynamic typing and expressive syntax.

- JavaScript's prototypal inheritance tends to feel strange to developers used to classical object-oriented programming. The main advantages are that it's dynamic (you can add new properties to prototypes and objects after they're created); there is no *diamond problem* (you never have ambiguities due to multiple ancestors); and it's simpler to just do what you want without rigid structures. We've seen that Three.js uses an inheritance pattern; you can also use OOP patterns in your code, and it helps to be aware of JavaScript's strengths in this regard instead of fighting with its weaknesses.

Using Grunt (`http://gruntjs.com/`) is strongly recommended to simplify your publishing and testing workflow because it helps minimize the amount of time between making a change and testing it in action. Grunt is a command-line tool that executes predetermined tasks, so you can use it to easily perform other publishing steps. For example, production code should be minified, concatenated, and checked for syntax errors, which Grunt can do using the UglifyJS and JSHint projects. If your project is open source, big enough, or has enough people to need separate documentation, JSDuck (`https://github.com/senchalabs/jsduck`) is a useful tool to automatically generate it from code comments (and Grunt supports it too). You can find a great tutorial on getting started with Grunt at `http://flippinawesome.org/2013/07/01/building-a-javascript-library-with-grunt-js/`.

Existing workflows and level development

Few changes should be needed to studios' existing game development pipelines in order to produce Three.js-based games. Some programmers may not even need to learn JavaScript if they're not already familiar with it since many languages compile to JavaScript. Existing processes can be maintained for testing and producing as well as for developing pitches, concepts, storyboards, models, textures, sounds, and other resources. The biggest challenge is in assembling those resources—building levels into Three.js scenes. There aren't amazing tools yet for designing levels for Three.js games that need them, partly because Three.js is a graphics library and games have a lot of custom requirements that are hard to generalize well for a single tool. Level editors tend to be tied pretty closely to the game engine and the classes it provides.

The original Three.js author has created a scene editor that you can try at `http://mrdoob.github.io/three.js/editor/`. It is useful for small projects, but quickly becomes unwieldy for big ones (especially when multiple people need to work on a project at the same time). Also, the scene editor can't handle custom objects such as spawn points, so if you use it, at least part of each level will need to be defined in custom code.

As a result, if you need to create many levels or you need to do so visually, you will probably need to build your own scene layout tool. There are a few ways you could do this. First, the Three.js scene editor is part of the Three.js project (in the `editor` folder), so you could start with that and edit it. Second, you could try writing an exporter for an existing level development tool or a converter for its save files, then writing a custom Three.js loader. Third, you could try writing your own tool from scratch. The good news on that front is that once you've written one, you can use it again in other projects.

> Clearly, writing reusable components is helpful if you're going to build more than one Three.js project. Before writing your own components, you may want to check out two Three.js helper libraries by *Jerome Etienne*: an extension system called **tQuery** and a series of utilities called **THREEx**, available at `http://jeromeetienne.github.io/tquery/` and `http://jeromeetienne.github.io/threex/`, respectively.

Voxel.js (`http://voxeljs.com/`) is a good example of a game engine with its own level editor. It also has a bunch of modules (including a multiplayer module) that you can plug in. It's designed for Minecraft-style games, but you might be able to use it as a starting point for other large-scale projects.

Summary

In this chapter, we learned about designing and developing high-quality games for the Web. We covered aspects of game design and development that are unique to the Web, and how Three.js supports them; important performance considerations; and basic client-server and lock-step networking.

You are now prepared to embrace the next generation of gaming. Congratulations!

Index

U

UDP 93
unlit 21
updateAnimation() method 69
update function 45
update() method 38, 54, 55, 58

V

Vector3 instance 43
VERTICAL_UNIT variable 47
vertices property 15
visible property 72
voxel collision 57
Voxel.js
  URL 97

W

Web
  game, designing for 81-83

WebGL 5
WebGLRenderer() method 34, 35, 72
Web Performance Optimization (WPO) 84
Web Sockets API
  URL 93
width attribute 9, 88
wireframeLinewidth option 23
wireframe option 23

X

x property 11

Y

yaw 49
y property 11

Z

z property 11

Thank you for buying
Game Development with Three.js

About Packt Publishing

Packt, pronounced 'packed', published its first book "*Mastering phpMyAdmin for Effective MySQL Management*" in April 2004 and subsequently continued to specialize in publishing highly focused books on specific technologies and solutions.

Our books and publications share the experiences of your fellow IT professionals in adapting and customizing today's systems, applications, and frameworks. Our solution based books give you the knowledge and power to customize the software and technologies you're using to get the job done. Packt books are more specific and less general than the IT books you have seen in the past. Our unique business model allows us to bring you more focused information, giving you more of what you need to know, and less of what you don't.

Packt is a modern, yet unique publishing company, which focuses on producing quality, cutting-edge books for communities of developers, administrators, and newbies alike. For more information, please visit our website: www.packtpub.com.

About Packt Open Source

In 2010, Packt launched two new brands, Packt Open Source and Packt Enterprise, in order to continue its focus on specialization. This book is part of the Packt Open Source brand, home to books published on software built around Open Source licences, and offering information to anybody from advanced developers to budding web designers. The Open Source brand also runs Packt's Open Source Royalty Scheme, by which Packt gives a royalty to each Open Source project about whose software a book is sold.

Writing for Packt

We welcome all inquiries from people who are interested in authoring. Book proposals should be sent to author@packtpub.com. If your book idea is still at an early stage and you would like to discuss it first before writing a formal book proposal, contact us; one of our commissioning editors will get in touch with you.

We're not just looking for published authors; if you have strong technical skills but no writing experience, our experienced editors can help you develop a writing career, or simply get some additional reward for your expertise.

Learn HTML5 by Creating Fun Games

ISBN: 978-1-84969-602-9   Paperback: 374 pages

Learn one of the most popular markup languages by creating simple yet fun games

1. Learn the basics of this emerging technology and have fun doing it

2. Unleash the new and exciting features and APIs of HTML5

3. Create responsive games that can be played on a browser and on a mobile device

Torque 3D Game Development Cookbook

ISBN: 978-1-84969-354-7   Paperback: 380 pages

Over 80 practical recipes and hidden gems for getting the most out of the Torque 3D game engine

1. Clear step-by-step instruction and practical examples to advance your understanding of Torque 3D and all of its sub-systems

2. Explore essential topics such as graphics, sound, networking and user input

3. Helpful tips and techniques to increase the potential of your Torque 3D games

Please check **www.PacktPub.com** for information on our titles

Instant Raspberry Pi Gaming

ISBN: 978-1-78328-323-1   Paperback: 60 pages

Your guide to gaming on the Raspberry Pi, from classic arcade games to modern 3D adventures

1. Learn something new in an Instant! A short, fast, focused guide delivering immediate results

2. Play classic and modern video games on your new Raspberry Pi computer

3. Learn how to use the Raspberry Pi app store

4. Written in an easy-to-follow, step-by-step manner that will have you gaming in no time

HTML5 Game Development with ImpactJS

ISBN: 978-1-84969-456-8   Paperback: 304 pages

A step-by-step guide to developing your own 2D games

1. A practical hands-on approach to teach you how to build your own game from scratch

2. Learn to incorporate game physics

3. How to monetize and deploy to the web and mobile platforms

Please check **www.PacktPub.com** for information on our titles